# DINOSAURS

igloobooks

Published in 2018
by Igloo Books Ltd
Cottage Farm
Sywell
NN6 0BJ
www.igloobooks.com

SHE011 1217
2 4 6 8 10 9 7 5 3
ISBN 978-1-7867-0646-1

Printed and manufactured in China

# DINOSAURS

igloobooks

# CONTENTS

MYA - Million years ago
BYA - Billion years ago

In the text, some words have been highlighted in **bold**. You will find more information about what these mean in the glossary.

5

# DINOSAUR TIMELINE

**Massive volcanic eruptions cause mass extinctions, wiping out 90% of marine life and 70% of land life!**

**First dinosaurs evolve. They are mostly fairly small – no more than 20 ft (6 m), bipedal, and fast moving.**
**Marine reptiles like Icthyosaurs and Plesiosaurs also evolve at this time.**

**Dinosaurs dominant. First mammals evolve.**

Mesozoic era

248 MYA – 65 MYA

| Triassic period | Jurassic period |
|---|---|
| 248 MYA – 206 MYA | 206 MYA – 144 MYA |

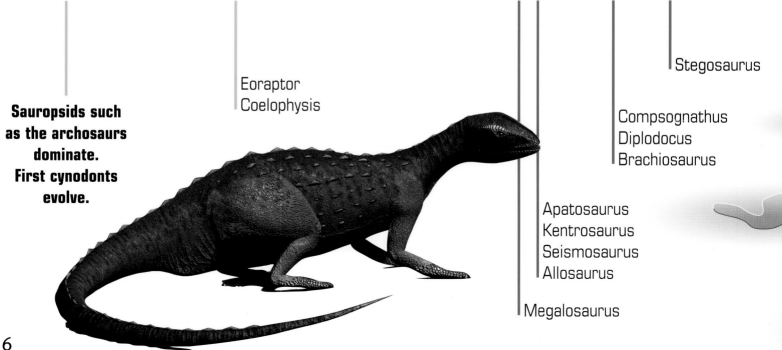

**Sauropsids such as the archosaurs dominate.**
**First cynodonts evolve.**

Eoraptor
Coelophysis

Stegosaurus

Compsognathus
Diplodocus
Brachiosaurus

Apatosaurus
Kentrosaurus
Seismosaurus
Allosaurus

Megalosaurus

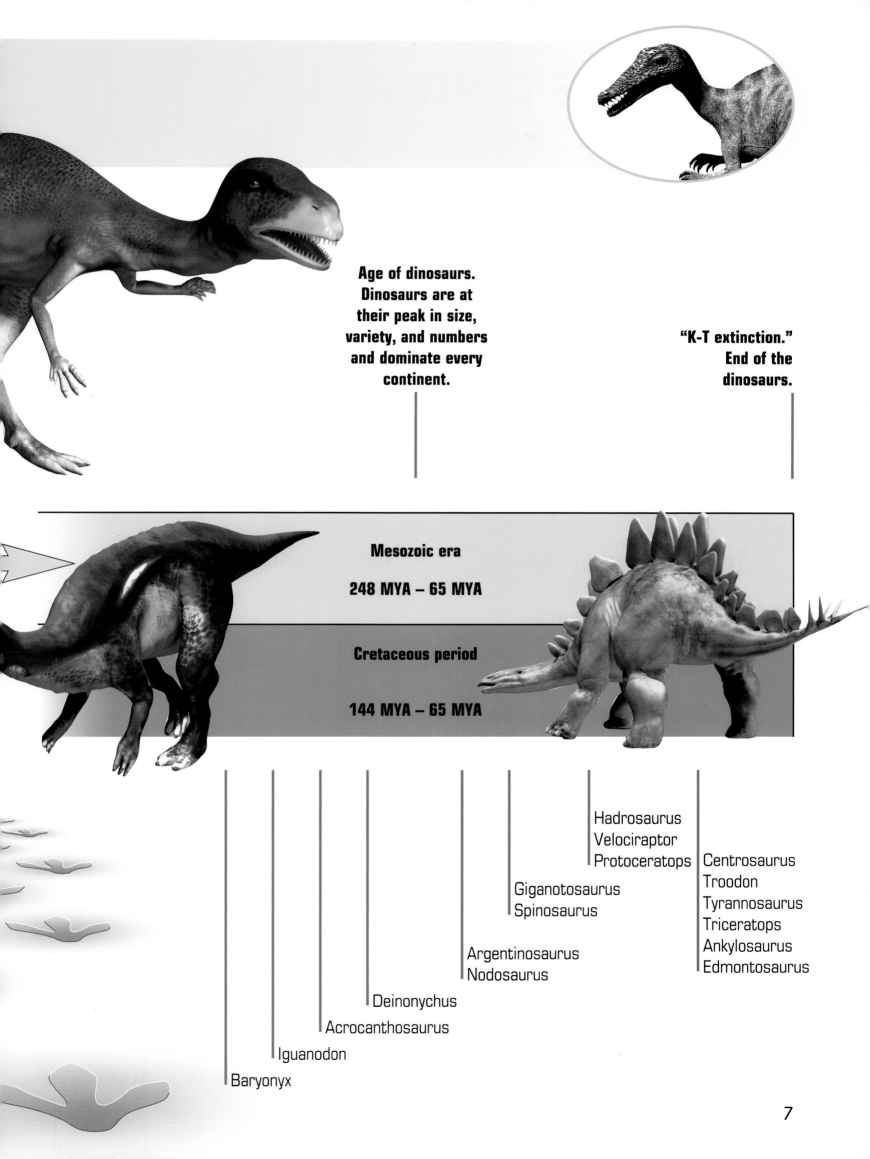

**Age of dinosaurs.
Dinosaurs are at
their peak in size,
variety, and numbers
and dominate every
continent.**

**"K-T extinction."
End of the
dinosaurs.**

**Mesozoic era**

**248 MYA – 65 MYA**

**Cretaceous period**

**144 MYA – 65 MYA**

Hadrosaurus
Velociraptor
Protoceratops

Centrosaurus
Troodon
Tyrannosaurus
Triceratops
Ankylosaurus
Edmontosaurus

Giganotosaurus
Spinosaurus

Argentinosaurus
Nodosaurus

Deinonychus

Acrocanthosaurus

Iguanodon

Baryonyx

# WHAT ARE DINOSAURS?

Dinosaurs were a kind of prehistoric reptile. They ruled the Earth for more than 150 million years, during a period of time called the Mesozoic era. The first dinosaur appeared on Earth about 230 million years ago. They all died out about 65 million years ago.

Everything we know about the dinosaurs comes from the fossilized remains of their bones (and sometimes impressions of their skin, or footprints). This means scientists have very little to go on when they try to work out how dinosaurs lived. We cannot tell from fossils what color a dinosaur's skin was, or what their voices sounded like. It is hard to tell how they behaved.

## Some dinosaur myths

### All dinosaurs were huge

Many were middle-sized or small. The smallest known dinosaur is Compsognathus (see page 30), which was only the size of a chicken.

### All giant prehistoric animals were dinosaurs

Many other types of animal shared the Mesozoic era with the dinosaurs.
Pterosaurs flew, and marine reptiles like the ichthyosaurs swam in the oceans.

## Some dinosaurs could fly, or swim

All dinosaurs lived on land. The pterosaurs and ichthyosaurs were not dinosaurs. Many scientists think that dinosaurs did eventually fly, though — by evolving into birds!

## Dinosaurs were the biggest animals that ever lived

Although a plant-eating dinosaur called Argentinosaurus (see page 42) was the largest ever land animal, it was not as massive as a modern day giant, the blue whale.

Scientists have named about 800 kinds of dinosaurs so far, and there must be many more fossils to find. New finds are made today almost every month – of course, not all of these are new species.

Most dinosaurs laid eggs and were cold-blooded. Apart from that, they were widely different in size, shape, and speed. Some were **herbivores** and some **carnivores**. Some moved on all fours (these are called **quadrupeds**) and some on just their back legs (these are called **bipeds**).

Scientific detectives called **paleontologists** study the fossil remains to learn as much as they can.

The name dinosaur means "terrible lizard." It comes from two Greek words: *deinos*, (terrifying) and *sauros* (lizard). The name was invented by Sir Richard Owen in 1842 (above left). Before that, people did not realize dinosaurs had once existed.

# MEGA FACTS

- **Largest – Argentinosaurus, 115-130 ft (35–40m) long**

- **Smallest – Compsognathus, weighed 8 lb (3.6kg), and was only 28 in. (70 cm) long**

- **Widest – Ankylosaurus, 5 ft (1.5 m) wide**

- **Longest neck – Mamenchisaurus, neck was 33 ft (10 m) long**

- **Fastest – Ornithomiminee, ran at 40–53 mph (64–85 km/h)**

- **First discovered – Iguanodon, found 1822**

- **Oldest – Eoraptor, lived 227 million years ago**

# ICHTHYOSAURUS

## Aquatic hunter/killer

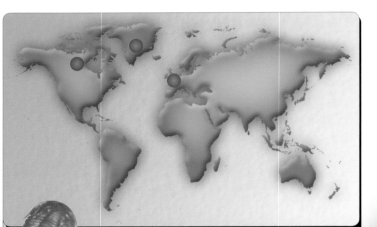

### FOSSIL FACTS
**Ichthyosaurus fossils have been found in England, Germany, Greenland, and Canada. The first was found in England in the early 19th century.**

Ichthyosaurus evolved from reptiles, but could swim like fish. It swam by moving its powerful tails from side to side. Since it needed to breathe air periodically, it probably lived close to the surface of the sea. It breathed through nostrils on the top of the head, near the top of the snout. Its long snout was packed with conical, pointed teeth.

### Appearance

Ichthyosaurus means "fish lizard." It was named in 1818 by Charles König from the British Museum. It is not a true dinosaur but a dolphin-like marine reptile. Ichthyosaurus lived from the early Jurassic period to the early Cretaceous period – around 206 to 140 million years ago.

| Permian period | Triassic period | Jurassic period | Cretaceous period |
|---|---|---|---|
| .90-248 million years ago) | (248-176 million years ago) | (176-130 million years ago) | (130-66 million years ago) |

## Reproduction and diet

Ichthyosaurus was smooth-skinned and streamlined, and had limbs (flippers) like large paddles to balance it in the water – the front "paddles" were twice as large as the back ones. Its eyes were unusually large, and surrounded by a strong ring of bone. A fish-like tail helped propel it, and a dorsal fin provided extra balance.

Ichthyosaurus gave birth to live young – we know this because fossils have been found showing baby Ichthyosaurus bones in the abdomen of adults. Fossils have also helped us learn about the diet of Ichthyosaurus – the hard hooks found on the tentacles of squid cannot be digested and so remained in the belly; one fossil of an Ichthyosaurus showed it had swallowed at least 1,500 squid while alive.

The first complete Ichthyosaurus fossil remains were found at Lyme Regis, England, by a girl called Mary Anning, in the early 19th century. Mary Anning made a living from collecting, studying, and selling fossils.

# MEGA FACTS

- Most were around 6 ft (2 m) long, though some were as big as 30 ft (9 m). An average weight for these dolphin-like creatures was 200 lb (90 kg).

- We know Ichthyosaurus must have moved fast to hunt its prey, because the remains of a fast-swimming fish called Pholidophorus have been found in fossilized Ichthyosaurus droppings. It could swim at speeds of up to 25 mph (40 km/h).

- Ichthyosaurus skeletons found at Holzmaden (Germany) were so well preserved that scientists could see outlines of skin as well as bones.

- In 2000, an Ichthyosaurus skeleton, believed to be almost a perfect specimen, was revealed as a fake when it was cleaned. It had been made in the Victorian age from the bones of two different creatures and some bones made out of plaster.

*Icthyosaurus fossil*

### Dinosaur Data

| | |
|---|---|
| PRONUNCIATION: | IK-THEE-OH-**SAWR**-US |
| SUBORDER: | ICHTHYOSAURIA |
| FAMILY: | ICHTHYOSAURIDAE |
| DESCRIPTION: | OCEAN-DWELLING PREDATOR |
| FEATURES: | ENORMOUS EYES, FOUR CRESCENT-SHAPED FLIPPERS, DORSAL FIN |
| DIET: | FISH, OCTOPUS AND OTHER SEA-DWELLING CREATURES |

# ELASMOSAURUS

## Long-necked marine reptile

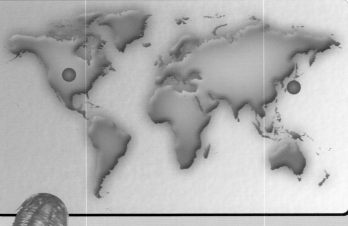

**FOSSIL FACTS**
Elasmosaurus fossils have been found in North America and Japan. The first was found in 1868.

Elasmosaurus was named by Edward Drinker Cope, who discovered the first fossil. Unfortunately, when Cope assembled his Elasmosaurus skeleton for display, he placed the head on the wrong end! His rivals soon pointed out his mistake, and made fun of him for it for the rest of his career.

### Appearance

The neck of Elasmosaurus contained more than 70 **vertebrae**. Elasmosaurus was the largest of a type of marine reptile called **plesiosaurs**. It had a large body, four long, broad paddles for limbs, and a small head with sharp, interlocking teeth.

Elasmosaurus means "thin-plated lizard" – the name refers to the plate-like bones in the creature's pelvic girdle. It lived 88–65 million years ago and swam in the great inland sea that covered much of the western part of North America in those times. Its body was dwarfed by its long thin neck and shorter tail.

## Dinosaur Data

| | |
|---|---|
| PRONUNCIATION: | EE-**LAZ**-MOH-SAWR-US |
| SUBORDER: | PLESIOSAURIOID |
| FAMILY: | ELASMOSAURIDAE |
| DESCRIPTION: | HUGE, SLOW-SWIMMING MARINE REPTILE |
| FEATURES: | EXTREMELY LONG NECK, TINY HEAD |
| DIET: | FISH AND OTHER SMALL MARINE CREATURES |

The long neck may have enabled Elasmosaurus to feed in a number of different ways.

It may have floated along on the surface, stretching down to the sea bottom to catch fish and other marine creatures. It could also make attacks upward at shoals of fish while its body was much lower down in the water. It could move slowly and stealthily toward them, then attack with a quick darting movement. The small size of its head and its narrow neck meant it could only eat and swallow smaller creatures. Elasmosaurus fossils have been found with rounded pebbles in their stomachs – perhaps they swallowed these to aid their digestion or to help them sink further down into the water.

Elasmosaurus is believed to have been a very slow swimmer. It would have traveled long distances to find safe mating and breeding grounds.

## Reproduction

For a long time, it was assumed that Elasmosaurus laid eggs like most reptiles, crawling ashore to lay its eggs on land. However, many scientists now think that Elasmosaurus gave birth to live young, which it raised until they could look after themselves in the predator-filled ocean. Elasmosaurus may have traveled together in small groups to protect their young.

# MEGA FACTS

- About 46 ft (14 m) long, Elasmosaurus was the longest of the plesiosaurs.

- Pictures often show Elasmosaurus holding its head high above the surface of the water at the end of its long neck. Actually, gravity would have made it impossible for it to lift much more than its head above water.

- Elasmosaurus, with its long snake-like neck, is one of the candidates for the Loch Ness Monster (see page 21).

# KRONOSAURUS

## Giant short-necked marine reptile

Kronosaurus means "Kronos's lizard." It had a short neck, four flippers, a huge head with powerful jaws, and a short, pointed tail.

Kronosaurus was a marine reptile called a pliosaur (a type of **plesiosaur**). It was heavier, faster, and fiercer than most plesiosaurs. It lived in the seas that covered parts of Australia, and breathed air. It swam with four powerful paddle-like flippers and may have been able to climb out onto land and move around a little. It probably had to leave water to lay its eggs in nests it would dig in the sand.

### Diet

Kronosaurus ate other sea creatures such as ammonites and squid. Rounded teeth at the back of its powerful jaws enabled Kronosaurus to crunch up tough shells and crush bone.

The fossilized remains of turtles and even smaller plesiosaurs have been found in the stomachs of Kronosaurus fossils, and long-necked plesiosaur skeletons have been found with Kronosaurus-like toothmarks on the bones. Like Elasmosaurus (see page 12), small stones have been found in Kronosaurus stomachs which might have helped them grind up their food during digestion.

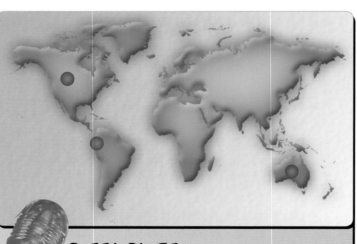

*Kronosaurus skeleton*

### FOSSIL FACTS
**Kronosaurus fossils have been found in Australia and Columbia – the first were found in Queensland, Australia, by A. Crombie in 1889.**

*Kronosaurus*

## Dinosaur Data

| PRONUNCIATION: | CROW-NO-SAWR-US |
| --- | --- |
| DESCRIPTION: | POWERFUL AQUATIC PREDATOR |
| FEATURES: | HUGE HEAD, POWERFUL JAWS |
| DIET: | CARNIVORE; ATE OTHER MARINE CREATURES |

Kronosaurus may have been able to 'scent' under water for its prey – it had internal nostrils where water could enter, and external ones farther back on the top of its skull for water to exit. While the water passed from one set to the other, scent particles could be detected.

## Appearance

Kronosaurus had an enormous head as skulls have been found measuring 10 ft (3 m). As their whole body length is believed to be only around

30 ft (9 m), this means their head took up a third of it!

It was originally thought to be much longer, earning it the title of 'largest ever plesiosaur', but recent studies have led scientists to downsize their image of Kronosaurus. The team of scientists who mounted the first specimen for display had to fill in many 'gaps' in the skeleton – they gave their mounted Kronosaurus too many vertebrae and so made it longer than it should have been.

# MEGA FACTS

- Fast and fierce – one of the top predators of the ancient ocean.

- Some of Kronosaurus' teeth were 10 in. (25 cm) long, although much of this length was embedded in the jawbone.

- When Kronosaurus fossils were first discovered in 1889, they were believed to come from an ichthyosaur. Kronosaurus did not get a name of its own until 1924.

- When the first Kronosaurus skeleton was assembled, the specimen was in such a bad state that the team had to fill in many details using plaster and their own imagination. This led to the creature being nicknamed the "Plasterosaurus!"

15

# MOSASAURUS

## Giant aquatic predator

Mosasaurus is named after the River Meuse near Maastricht (Netherlands), where the first fossil specimen was found (*mosa-*, the Latin name for the Meuse River, and *-saurus* for lizard). It was given this name in 1822.

Mosasaurus was a gigantic meat-eating reptile that lived 70–65 million years ago. It frequented shallow seas, as it still needed to breathe air. It had a long, streamlined body, four paddle-like limbs, and a long, powerful tail. It was a powerful swimmer, between 39 ft (12 m) and 58 ft (17.6 m) in length. Its large head had huge jaws (up to 5 ft (1.45 m) long). These jaws could open up to 3 ft (1 m) thanks to the Mosasaurus' peculiar jaw design.

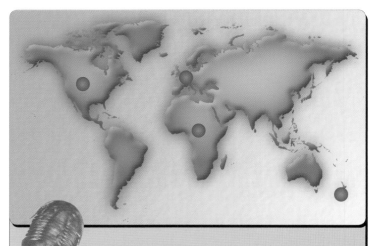

### Dinosaur Data

| | |
|---|---|
| PRONUNCIATION: | MOES-AH-SAWR-US |
| DESCRIPTION: | GIANT, SWIFT-MOVING AQUATIC PREDATOR |
| FEATURES: | SPECIALLY HINGED JAWS, LONG AND POWERFUL TAIL |
| DIET: | SHARKS, FISH, AND OTHER MARINE REPTILES |

### FOSSIL FACTS

Fossils have been found in North America, Africa, New Zealand, and Europe. The first Mosasaurus fossil was found in a quarry in the Netherlands in 1780.

## Jaws

Mosasaurus had very special jaws. It had an extra joint halfway along the jaw, which let it handle huge mouthfuls of food. Its lower jaw could drop lower and also move out sideways – much like snakes which can "unhinge" their jaws to swallow very large pieces of food like whole rats. Monitor lizards, to which Mosasaurus is directly related, still have this special jaw. Set into this jaw were rows of backward-curving teeth. Just as with sharks, when one tooth wore down, another grew in its place.

## Diet

The preserved stomach contents of Mosasaur fossils show them to have eaten sharks, bony fish, turtles, and other marine reptiles.

## Skeleton

Mosasaurus had about 100 vertebrae in its back (four times as many as humans), each joined to the next by a flexible ball-and-socket joint. This would have allowed Mosasaurus to move in the water like an eel. It was one of the most ferocious aquatic predators of its time.

## Reproduction

Scientists cannot agree as to whether Mosasaurus came up on land to lay its eggs in sand (like turtles), or gave birth to live young in the water.

Mosasaurus fossils were some of the earliest dinosaur fossils to be discovered, and because of them, scientists began to discuss the possibility that such fossils belonged to species which had actually died out.

# MEGA FACTS

- Mosasaurus is directly related to monitor lizards.

- Recent studies suggest the first Mosasaurus specimen was actually a partial skull found as early as 1766, near St. Pietersburg, near Maastricht.

- In 1795, a Mosasaurus skull was traded to the occupying French army for 600 bottles of wine! It sits in a Paris museum.

- Like a Tylosaurus, a Mosasaurus rarely bit off more than it could chew – it could unhinge its special jaw to swallow huge prey such as sharks.

*Mosasaurus skeleton*

# OPHTHALMOSAURUS

## Huge-eyed aquatic hunter

### FOSSIL FACTS
Fossils have been found in Europe and Argentina. The earliest find was made by British scientist Harry Seeley in 1874.

Ophthalmosaurus means "eye lizard" in Greek. The name comes from its dinner-plate sized eyes – Ophthalmosaurus had the largest eyes relative to its size of any vertebrate, measuring up to 9 in. (23 cm) across. These eyes took up almost the whole depth of its skull on each side. Fossil remains show a ring of strong bone surrounding these eyes – these would have supported the eye against water pressure, suggesting that Ophthalmosaurus could dive into deep, dark water after prey or to hide from predators.

It may well have been a night hunter, as its large eyes were well adapted for low light conditions and would have helped it to spot the squid that were its favorite prey. (Large eyes can house more light-gathering cells, and so are more effective in the dark.)

## Appearance

Although it was perfectly adapted for living in the water, Ophthalmosaurus needed to breathe air, like a dolphin or whale does. It was not a true dinosaur, but a marine reptile. Swift and supple, its 20 ft (6 m) long body resembled

### Dinosaur Data

| | |
|---|---|
| PRONUNCIATION: | OFF-THAL-MOH-SAW-RUS |
| FAMILY: | ICHTHYSAURIDAE |
| DESCRIPTION: | DOLPHIN-LIKE HUNTER |
| FEATURES: | ENORMOUS EYES |
| DIET: | SQUID AND FISH |

that of a dolphin, tear-shaped with a dorsal fin. Its front fins were more developed than its back ones; Ophthalmosaurus probably propelled itself with its tail and steered with its front fins. The skull took up about 3 ft (1 m) of its 20 ft (6 m) body.

## The bends

Although it could dive to great depths, Ophthalmosaurus may have paid a price for doing so. Fossil evidence shows clear signs of what modern deep-sea divers call the bends – when a diver ascends too quickly, decompressed nitrogen in the blood forms painful bubbles that can damage tissue and even bone. Ophthalmosaurus remains show signs of the animal having suffered in exactly this way, leaving visible depressions in the joints and limb bones.

## Reproduction

Ophthalmosaurus could not get onto land to lay eggs, instead giving birth to live young in the water. Their young – which we call "pups" – were born tail first, to prevent them from drowning. We know this because fossils survive of females in the act of giving birth.

Numbers of young ranged from two to 11, although it seems to have been most normal to give birth to only two or three at a time.

*Ophthalmosaurus and Stenosaurus*

# MEGA FACTS

- Ophthalmosaurus lived 165–150 million years ago.

- May have been capable of diving to depths of 3 miles (4.9 km); calculations show it would still have had clear sight this far down.

- Had an almost toothless jaw, specially adapted for catching squid and fish.

# PLESIOSAURUS

## Four-paddled marine reptile

**FOSSIL FACTS**
The first fossils were found in 1821 in England by Mary Anning.

The name Plesiosaurus means "near to lizard" or "near lizard" and comes from the Greek words *plesios* (near to) and *sauros* (lizard). The name was coined by H. T. De La Beche and William D. Conybeare in 1821.

### Appearance

Plesiosaurus was one of a number of marine reptiles that lived at the same time as the dinosaurs. Plesiosaurus was characterized by a long, thin neck, tiny head and wide bodies. Plesiosaurus was about 7 ft 6 in. (2.3 m) long and may have weighed around 198 lb (90 kg).

Plesiosaurus lived in the open oceans but still needed to breathe air; this means it would had to have come to the surface regularly to breathe – much like whales and dolphins do.

We believe it swam using its four flippers in pairs, one pair "rowing" and the other pair moving in an up-down motion with the tail being used for steering. No other creatures are known to swim in this way.

### Reproduction

Scientists had speculated that, like the turtle, it dragged itself up onto sandy beaches to lay its eggs, which it would bury in the sand before heading back to the ocean again.

*Plesiosaurus skeleton*

However, the current theory is that the Plesiosaurus gave birth to live young in the oceans. This would certainly have made things easier on the baby Plesiosaurus as it wouldn't have to hatch and then scurry down the beach to reach the relative safety of the ocean like baby sea turtles.

### Diet

Fossilized remains found in the stomachs of Plesiosaurus fossils show that they ate fish and other swimming animals. We know they also swallowed small stones! We believe this was either to help break up their food or to help weigh them down for diving deeper into the ocean.

The first Plesiosaurus fossils were found on the **Jurassic Coast**. In 2004 a fully intact fossilized juvenile Plesiosaurus was found about 31 miles (50 km) north of where the first Plesiosaurus was found!

# MEGA FACTS

- The first Plesiosaurus fossil was found long before the first dinosaur fossil was found.

- A Plesiosaurus is one of the creatures mentioned in Jules Verne's *Journey to the Centre of the Earth* – it battles an Icthyosaur (see page 10).

- Many people believe that the Loch Ness Monster could be a Plesiosaurus. However, this seems unlikely as the cold water of the loch would not support a cold-blooded creature like the Plesiosaurus and the loch only formed 10,000 years ago – while Plesiosaurus became extinct millions of years ago.

## Dinosaur Data

| | |
|---|---|
| PRONUNCIATION: | PLEE-SEE-O-SAWR-UHS |
| SUBORDER: | PLESIOSAUROID |
| FAMILY: | PLESIOSAURIDAE |
| DESCRIPTION: | ROUGHLY MAN-SIZED AQUATIC PREDATOR |
| FEAUTURES: | LONG SINUOUS NECK, FOUR PADDLE-LIKE FINS, TINY HEAD WITH LONG SHARP TEETH |
| DIET: | FISH AND SMALLER AQUATIC ANIMALS |

# ATTACK AND DEFENSE

Dinosaurs attacked each other, defended themselves, and competed for leadership within groups. Even though some of the dinosaurs could be deadly, most of them were peaceful **herbivores** that never attacked. Herbivore dinosaurs usually tried to escape before fighting. Their means of attack and defense were either used to defend themselves or to compete for food, space, and a mate within their group.

## Defense

Dinosaurs defended themselves by disguise, herding together, or fighting back. Some of the small plant eaters found that running away was often the best way to stay alive! Good hearing and eyesight was essential for fast running at the first sign of danger.

Means of attack and defense ranged from the active use of teeth, claws, and horns to passive means like camouflage and armor.

Many plant eaters protected vulnerable body parts, such as necks and spines, with bony neck frills, tooth-snapping bone studs, and plates, and many had a sharp claw, horn or spike for swift counterattack.

Some dinosaurs were large enough for their size alone to be a defense. There were no other predators big enough to tackle an adult.

Dinosaurs that lived in herds for protection competed with each other for social order, for example to see who would be the leader. The fighting didn't usually end in death or serious injury though, because the dinosaurs didn't want to reduce the size of the herd.

## Attack

Dinosaurs which were **carnivores** had ferocious weapons which could kill other dinosaurs, such as sharp teeth or powerful legs for speed and leaping attacks.

*Acrocanthosaurus*

Daspletosaurus used its powerful jaw armed with a large number of sharp, strong teeth. Deinonychus was very agile and used its front and hind claws to hang onto and injure other dinosaurs.

*Scelidosaurus*

Therizinosaurus had giant claws, which it would wave at an enemy to show the size of them. Troodon, a small flat-footed predator, had 3-D vision eyes which probably allowed it to stalk small mammals that came out at dusk, when others could not see in the dark.

*Therizinosaurus*

Allosaurus (see page 34), when hunting alone, would have attacked small to medium-sized dinosaurs, but when pack-hunting several Allosaurus would have been capable of bringing down very large dinosaurs such as Diplodocus (see page 44).

The terrifying Postosuchus was a hunter who could attack and kill almost any animal of its time. It hunted other large animals by a combination of stealth and ambush so that it could take its prey by surprise.

*Compsognathus*

# TYRANNOSAURUS REX

## King of the tyrant lizards

Powerful hind legs and very large feet would have enabled Tyrannosaurus Rex to walk and, probably even run for long distances in search of food. Even though its hands were tiny, they were armed with savage claws for ripping and tearing flesh from its prey. Its sharp teeth allowed it to rip flesh from a carcass and it could crush and grind the bones with its powerful jaw. It was also an opportunistic feeder and would also scavenge for dead animals whenever fresh food was in short supply.

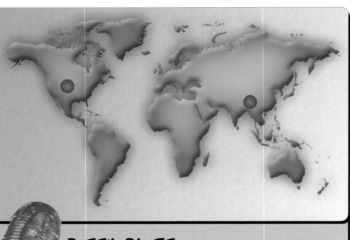

### FOSSIL FACTS
**Fossils have been found in several places in the USA and also in Mongolia.**

Tyrannosaurus Rex was one of the biggest and most powerful dinosaurs. It was first discovered in 1902 and was named in 1905.

Tyrannosaurus Rex probably lived in family groups. Smaller dinosaurs would have been subjected to its fierce and often fatal attacks. Large Tyrannosaurus Rex bite marks have been identified in the fossils of other dinosaurs.

### Dinosaur Data

| | |
|---|---|
| PRONUNCIATION: | TIE-RAN-O-SAW-RUS REX |
| SUBORDER: | THERAPODA |
| FAMILY: | TYRANNOSAUROIDEA |
| DESCRIPTION: | LARGE, POWERFUL CARNIVORE |
| FEATURES: | DOMINANT PREDATOR |
| DIET: | HUNTED AND SCAVENGED |

## Appearance

Tyrannosaurus Rex was 15–20 ft (4.5–6 m) tall and would have been able to see through the tops of the trees in the swampy forest it lived in.

The most recently discovered Tyrannosaurus Rex fossil was found in South Dakota in 1990; she's been called Sue after the woman who found her and is now on display in the Field Museum in Chicago.

# MEGA FACTS

- Over 39 ft (12 m) long from the nose to the end of tail.

- Could move at 10–30 mph (16–48 km/h).

- Powerful jaw of 58 serrated teeth each 6 in. (15 cm) long which regrew when they were damaged.

- 200 bones in a full Tyrannosaurus skeleton – roughly the same number as a human.

- Fossil Sue was auctioned at Sotheby's for $7.6 million in 1997.

Dinosaur experts continue to search for new fossils and examine those already found to learn more about how this giant **carnivore** lived and died.

25

# GIGANOTOSAURUS

## Giant southern lizard (new king of the carnivores)

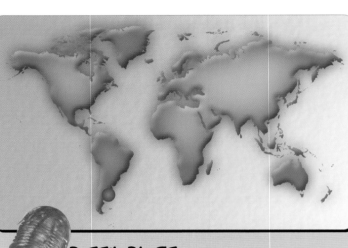

**FOSSIL FACTS**
**Fossils have been found at various sites in Argentina (South America). The first was discovered by Ruben Carolini in Patagonia (Argentina) in 1994.**

Giganotosaurus means "Giant Southern Lizard." It was given its name in 1995 by Coria and Salgado.

Giganotosaurus lived at the same time as enormous plant-eating dinosaurs like Argentinosaurus (see page 42) which it could hunt and eat. Like Tyrannosaurus Rex (see page 24), which lived 30 million years later, it hunted in warm, swampy areas.

## Appearance

Giganotosaurus was 18 ft (5.5 m) high and measured up to 49 ft (15 m) long but is not the largest dinosaur of all time; Argentinosaurus, is the largest dinosaur at the moment, and there may be more that we have not discovered yet. In 2006, scientists suggested that Gigantosaurus has now been displaced as largest **carnivore** by Spinosaurus, based on a study of new finds.

Although larger than T-Rex, Giganotosaurus was more lightly built, and it is thought it could run quite fast. Its slender, pointed tail would have helped to balance it out as it ran, probably moving from side to side. It would also have helped Giganotosaurus make quick turns. From its skull, we know that it probably had a good sense of smell and excellent eyesight thanks to its large eyes.

Giganotosaurus walked on two legs, had a long slim tail, and had enormous jaws in its 6 ft (1.8 m) skull.

## Attacking prey

Those jaws were lined with serrated teeth, well adapted for slicing into flesh and up to 8 in. (20 cm) long.

It did not have the powerful crushing bite of T-Rex, and so would have attacked by slashing. It had three clawed fingers it could use to slash, or grasp with.

When hunting, it would probably have singled out dinosaurs that were young, or weak, or separated from the herd. Fossil evidence where several skeletons were found close together suggests that they may have hunted and lived in packs.

Giganotosaurs may have cooperated in tasks like hunting and protecting their young.

# MEGA FACTS

- Weighed as much as 125 people.

- Appeared in 3-D in the IMAX® film *Dinosaurs*. Also in the *Walking with Dinosaurs* special *Land of Giants*, in which a pack of Giganotosaurs bring down an Argentinosaurus.

- The biggest Giganotosaurus was over three feet longer and a ton heavier than "Sue," the largest known Tyrannosaurus Rex.

- May have hunted prey up to ten times its own size.

- Giganotosaurus had a skull the size of a bathtub, but its brain was only the size (and shape) of a banana.

**Note** This is not the same dinosaur as the African sauropod Gigantosaurus (different spelling) named by Seeley in 1869.

## Dinosaur Data

| | |
|---|---|
| PRONUNCIATION: | JIG-A-NOT-OH-SAWR-US |
| SUBORDER: | THERAPODA |
| FAMILY: | ALLOSAURIDAE |
| DESCRIPTION: | LARGE POWERFUL CARNIVORE |
| FEATURES: | DOMINANT PREDATOR |

# BARYONYX

## Fish-eating dinosaur

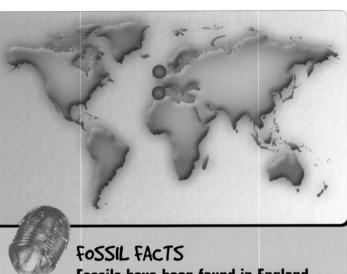

**FOSSIL FACTS**
**Fossils have been found in England and Spain. The first fossil was found by William Walker in 1983.**

Baryonyx means "heavy claw" and comes from the Greek words *bary* (heavy) and *onyx* (claw). It was named by Angela C. Milner and Alan J. Charig in 1987, because of the 12 in. (30 cm) long curved claw found on each of the creature's hands. So far only two Baryonyx fossils have been found.

## Appearance

Even though only two fossils have been found it has still been possible to learn a lot about this dinosaur because the first find was so complete. Baryonyx was about 31 ft (9.5 m) long, 16 ft (5 m) tall and probably weighed about 2.5 tons (2,500 kg). It had a long straight neck (unlike the

'S' shaped necks of other **therapods**) that supported a skull with a long jaw and many teeth, a long tail (which helped it to balance), two long back legs and two slightly shorter front legs, each of which had a 12 in. (30 cm) long curved claw.

The size and shape of Baryonyx's back legs suggest it would have been a fast runner as the thigh bone is relatively short compared to the calf. Baryonyx's neck would have been angled slightly downward.

## Teeth and diet

Baryonyx's teeth were very unusual for dinosaurs – the cutting edges were much finer.

This would have meant they were not well suited to tearing meat but would instead have been very good at holding prey in place. This suggested that Baryonyx was ideally suited for eating fish. Fossils of scales from a 3 ft (1 m) long fish called Lepidotes have been found in the stomach area of a Baronyx fossil. Scientists believe that Baryonyx would have waited on the banks or in shallow waters for fish to move past and may have used its large claws to scoop them out of the water. It could also have held its head underwater and snapped fish up directly as its nostrils were high enough up on its skull for it to have its jaws underwater and still be able to breathe.

# MEGA FACTS

- Baryonyx type name is Baryonyx Walkeri – named after the amateur fossil hunter William Walker, who found the first fossil.

- Baryonyx's upper jaw had a sharp angle near the snout, a feature seen in crocodiles that helps to prevent prey from escaping.

- Baryonyx was the first meat-eating dinosaur to be discovered in England and the first fish-eating dinosaur to be discovered anywhere.

## Dinosaur Data

| | |
|---|---|
| PRONUNCIATION: | BAR-EE-ON-IKS |
| SUBORDER: | THERAPODA |
| FAMILY: | SPINOSAURIDAE |
| DESCRIPTION: | LOW-SLUNG FISH-EATING DINOSAUR |
| FEATURES: | LONG STRAIGHT NECK, 96 SHARP TEETH WITH MICROSCOPIC SERRATIONS, 12 IN. CLAWS ON ITS HANDS. |
| DIET: | FISH; BARYONYX WAS A PISCIVORE AND WAS THE FIRST OF ONLY TWO FISH-EATING DINOSAURS TO BE DISCOVERED SO FAR (THE OTHER IS SUCHOMIMUS) |

# COMPSOGNATHUS

## Tiny, fleet-footed predator

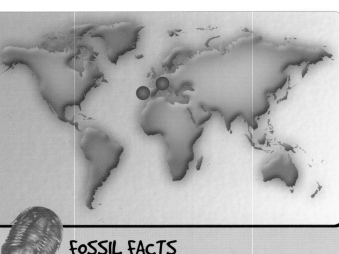

**FOSSIL FACTS**
Fossils have been found in France and Germany, and possibly Portugal. The first specimen was discovered in Bavaria, Germany, in the late 1850s by Dr. Oberndorfer.

Compsognathus means "elegant jaw" and comes from the Greek words *kompos* (elegant) and *gnathos* (jaw). It was named for the delicate bones of its lightlybuilt skull. It was given this name in 1859, by Johann A. Wagner.

Compsognathus was an early member of a group of dinosaurs called the **coelurosaurs** ("hollow-tail lizards"). Later members of the coelurosaur group included the most likely ancestors of birds. Compsognathus had hollow bones throughout its body. This made it very light and fast.

## Appearance

Compsognathus ran on its long, thin hind legs and had surprisingly short arms. It had a long tail to act as a counterbalance and to stabilize it during fast turns. Its head was small and pointed and it had a long, flexible neck. Its skull suggests it had good eyesight and was probably pretty intelligent. The characteristics of its skull

and legs tell us that Compsognathus was capable of rapid acceleration, high speed, flexibility, and quick reactions.

We know its size from two almost complete skeletons. Study of other partial skeletons gives a range of size from 28–56 in. (70–140 cm). It weighed only around 8 lb (3.6 kg) when fully-grown, and stood not much more than 1ft 6 in. (half a meter) tall.

**Palaeontologists** cannot agree over whether Compsognathus had two or three fingers on each hand. Either way, those slender fingers would have helped with grasping prey, which could then be swallowed whole or torn into pieces by tiny, sharp teeth.

## Habitat

At the time Compsognathus lived, water covered much of what is now France and southern Germany. Compsognathus lived on islands in this sea. Although very small, it was probably the largest predator where it lived – the small islands did not have enough vegetation to support large **herbivores**, which in turn meant there was no tempting prey for large **carnivores**.

# MEGA FACTS

- Compsognathus appeared in *Jurassic Park II* and *Jurassic Park III* as the vicious 'compys'. These films showed them hunting in packs, but in fact we have no idea whether they did this or not.

- Even fully grown, Compsognathus would weigh no more than a turkey.

- According to calculations made using the distance between fossilized footprints, Compsognathus could run at speeds up to 25 mph (40 km/h).

- The first fossil skeleton of this dinosaur that was found had the remains of a fast-running lizard called bavarisaurus in its stomach.

- In recent years the remains of even smaller dinosaurs have been found. These included the 18 in. (50 cm ) long plant-eating Micropachycephalosaurus, which as well as being the smallest dinosaur in the world also has the longest name!

- Evidence of feathers has yet to be discovered on a Compsognathus fossil.

## Dinosaur Data

| | |
|---|---|
| PRONUNCIATION: | KOMP-SOG-**NAY**-THUS *OR* KOMP-SO-**NATH**-US |
| SUBORDER: | THEROPODA |
| FAMILY: | COMPSOGNATHIDAE |
| DESCRIPTION: | BIPEDAL CARNIVORE |
| FEATURES: | HOLLOW BONES |
| DIET: | SMALL ANIMALS |

# VELOCIRAPTOR

## Swift and vicious bipedal carnivore

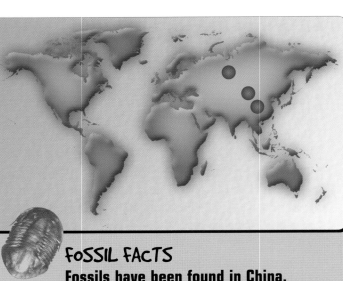

### FOSSIL FACTS
Fossils have been found in China, Mongolia, and Russia. The first Velociraptor fossils were found in 1914.

Velociraptor means "speedy thief." This carnivore lived in a desert-like environment around 70 million years ago, and may have hunted in packs, preying largely on **herbivores** like Hadrosaurus (see page 50).

### Appearance

It was about 5–6 ft (1.5–2 m), and stood on two legs. It had long arms and a long straight tail. Its strong jaws contained

around 80 sharp bladed teeth – some of the teeth were over 1 in. (2.5 cm) long. It possessed large eyes, which gave it excellent vision even in the dark.

Velociraptor had an enlarged second toe with a vicious oversized claw attached to it. These sickle-like claws could be raised off the ground while running or walking, then used once the Velociraptor launched an attack.

### Dinosaur Data

| | |
|---|---|
| PRONUNCIATION: | VUH-**LOSS**-IH-**RAP**-TOR |
| SUBORDER: | THERAPODA |
| FAMILY: | DROMAESORIDAE |
| DESCRIPTION: | SMALL, SWIFT CARNIVORE |
| FEATURES: | VERY INTELLIGENT, BIPEDAL |
| DIET: | HUNTED AND POSSIBLY SCAVENGED |

## The claw experiments

In 2005 Dr. Phil Manning performed experiments using a robotic claw designed to mimic the attack of a Velociraptor. The results showed that, against larger prey with tough skin, the claw would not have made wounds deep enough to kill quickly. The large claws were probably used to pierce and hold prey. Its razor-sharp teeth would then tear into the prey, causing as much blood loss as possible to vulnerable areas.

# MEGA FACTS

- Recent scientific thinking is that Velociraptor was very close to being birdlike, and may well have been covered in primitive feathers for warmth and display.

- Scientists believe a Velociraptor could leap up to 12 ft (3.6 m) to attack its prey.

- Velociraptor could run up to about 37 mph (60 km/h).

- They were probably warm-blooded to some degree.

- The Velociraptor had a very big brain compared to its body size, making it one of the most intelligent of the dinosaurs.

## Breathing

Some scientists now believe raptors could have had a way of breathing like modern birds. Birds store extra air in air sacs inside their hollow bones as well as using their lungs – this means they can extract oxygen from air much more efficiently than mammals. A comparison between bird anatomy and fossilized dinosaur remains revealed many similarities.

## Fossilized attack

An especially interesting fossil was discovered in 1971 in the Gobi Desert – it revealed a Velociraptor in mid-attack on a Protoceratops. The claws of the Velociraptor were buried in the body of the Protoceratops, its sickle claws close to where the jugular vein would have been – but the Protoceratops has the raptor's arm firmly in its jaws. Both seem to have died in a sudden sandstorm, or landslip, preserving their battle forever.

# ALLOSAURUS

## Dominant flesh eater

### FOSSIL FACTS
Fossils have been found in the western USA and (recently) in Europe. The first fossils were found in Colarado, USA.

very powerful arms. It also had large claws on its hands – one claw discovered was more than 11 ft (350 cm) long.

Allosaurus was light thanks to air sacs in its bones – this would have allowed it to run very fast, and also to leap at its prey, tear out a chunk with its teeth, and then leap away again.

Allosaurus means "different lizard", so named because its vertebrae (backbones) were different from those of all other dinosaurs. The first specimen was studied and named by Othniel C. March in 1877.

### Appearance

Allosaurus was between 23–39 ft (7–12 m) in length, 10–15 ft (3–4.5 m) tall and weighed 1–4 tons (1,000–4,500 kg). It had a huge head, long strong hind legs and

### Dinosaur Data

| | |
|---|---|
| PRONUNCIATION: | AL-UH-**SAWR**-US |
| SUBORDER: | THERAPODA |
| FAMILY: | ALLOSAURIDAE |
| DESCRIPTION: | BIPEDAL CARNIVORE |
| FEATURES: | HINGED JAW, BLUNT HORNS |
| DIET: | PLANT-EATING DINOSAURS |

| Permian period | Triassic period | Jurassic period | Cretaceous period |
|---|---|---|---|
| 90-248 million years ago) | (248-176 million years ago) | (176-130 million years ago) | (130-66 million years ago) |

Allosaurus was the most common large predator in North America 155–145 million years ago – so many fossil remains have been found in this area that some scientists suggest Allosaurus might have hunted in large packs.

## Skeletons

In 1991, a 95% complete skeleton of a young Allosaurus was discovered and named "Big Al." Big Al was 26 ft (8 m) in length and 19 of his bones showed signs of breakage or infection. He was discovered by a Swiss team led by Kirby Siber. The same team later excavated an even more impressive Allosaurus skeleton – the best preserved of its kind to date – which was promptly christened "Big Al 2."

## Attacking prey

Recently, more information has come to light about the way an Allosaurus attacked its prey. A scientist at Cambridge University (England) named Emily Rayfield created a computer model of Big Al's skull, using techniques usually used in engineering.

The model allowed her to calculate the force that Big Al's jaws would have needed to break the skull of a living creature. She concluded that Allosaurus actually had quite a weak bite.

The skull was also very light, but capable of withstanding massive upward force. Rayfield concluded that the Allosaur had actually attacked by opening its mouth wide and using powerful neck muscles to drive its upper jaw downward, slamming into its prey like an axe and tearing away hunks of flesh.

## MEGA FACTS

- Allosaurus jaws were able to "expand" to allow larger chunks of food to be swallowed.

- Allosaurus has been featured in several films.

- Footprint evidence suggests that Allosaurus hunted in packs, and may have raised its young in large nests.

- An Allosaurus could run at almost 37 mph (60 km/h).

# MEGALOSAURUS

## Huge bipedal

MEAT EATERS

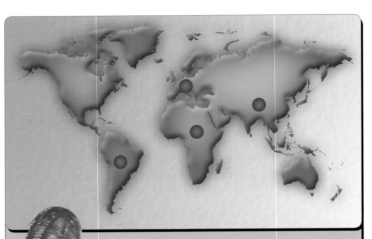

**FOSSIL FACTS**
**Fossils have been found in Europe, Asia, Africa, and South America.**

This **carnivore** grew to a length of 30 ft (9 m), a height of 12 ft (3.7 m). It was **bipedal**. It had a long tail to help balance out its heavy head.

Its back legs were much longer than its arms. The arms had hands that could have been used for grasping. The legs ended in four-toed feet (one toe was reversed, like all **therapod** dinosaurs). Both fingers and toes had strong, sharp claws.

## Diet

Megalosaurus was a powerful hunter, and could attack even the largest prey. It would have hunted plant-eating

Megalosaurus means "great lizard." It was named in 1824 and was the first dinosaur to be given a scientific name.

## Appearance

No complete skeleton has yet been discovered so we cannot be 100% certain of what it looked like.

Megalosaurus had a big head, and its curved teeth had saw edges well suited to eating meat. Its jaws were very powerful. It had small eyes with bony knobs over the top of them, and its head was held up by a strong, short neck.

## Dinosaur Data

| | |
|---|---|
| PRONUNCIATION: | MEG-UH-LOW-**SAWR**-US |
| SUBORDER: | THERAPODA |
| FAMILY: | MEGALOSAURIDAE |
| DESCRIPTION: | LARGE BIPEDAL CARNIVORE |
| FEATURES: | POWERFUL JAWS, BULKY BODY, LARGE HEAD |
| DIET: | OTHER DINOSAURS |

dinosaurs. It probably also scavenged from dead bodies as part of its diet.

## Movement

Megalosaurus waddled, rather like a duck, its tail swishing from side to side! Scientists have studied its fossilized footprints, which show that its feet pointed inwards as it walked.

There is fossil evidence to suggest Megalosaurus could actually put on quite a turn of speed when it had to. In 2002, scientists from the University of Cambridge (England) studied fossilized footprints left by Megalosaurus. For about 115 ft (35 m), the footprints looked different to the rest. They were about 10 ft (3 m) apart, and went in a straight line – it looked as if the dinosaur had been placing its feet almost directly beneath itself as it ran.

# MEGA FACTS

- Fossilized footprints made by Megalosaurus and another dinosaur called Cetiosaurus have been found in a section of limestone that covers a fifth of a square mile (half a square kilometer).

- In 1676, the thighbone of a Megalosaurus was found in England. Professors at Oxford University declared it was from a giant man!

- Megalosaurus was one of the more intelligent dinosaurs.

At the end of this 115 ft (35 m), the tracks began to change, showing the dinosaur slowing down. In few strides, the prints settled into a new pattern. The footprints were now only 4 ft (1.3 m) apart, and started to look 'pigeon-toed' (with the toes turned in). Using these tracks, scientists estimated that Megalosaurus could run at around 18 mph (29 km/h). It would usually have plodded along at around 4 mph (7 km/h).

# OVIRAPTOR PHILOCARATOPS

## Odd-looking omnivorous raptor

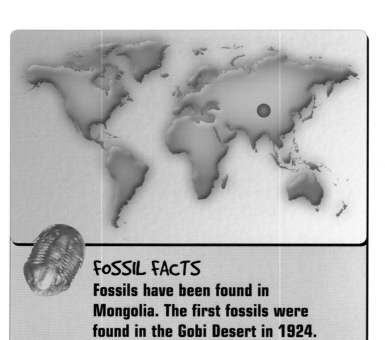

### FOSSIL FACTS
**Fossils have been found in Mongolia. The first fossils were found in the Gobi Desert in 1924.**

Oviraptor philoceratops means "egg thief, fond of horned dinosaurs."

Oviraptor was a small, fast-moving **biped** with long slender legs and short arms for grasping. At the ends of these arms were large three-fingered hands with claws up to 3 in. (8 cm) long. It had a flexible neck, a long tail, its powerful jaws were designed for crushing and its skull was almost parrot-shaped. On top of its snout was a thin bony crest, which seemed to change with age.

The shape of Oviraptor's head and mouth would have made it equipped for dealing with a variety of food. It was probably an **omnivore**, making up its diet from almost anything it could find – for example, meat, plants, eggs, insects, and shellfish. Omnivorous dinosaurs are very rare.

38

*Fossil*

# MEGA FACTS

- Oviraptor could run at about 43 mph (70 km/h).

- It was 6–8 ft (1.8–2.5 m) long and weighed about 80 lb (36 kg).

- If an Oviraptor sat on its eggs to keep them warm, that would mean it was warm-blooded. However, they may have sat on their eggs for other reasons, like protecting them.

- Its crest may have been used for mating display, or to distinguish between males and females.

- Oviraptors share many characteristics with birds, and may have been covered in feathers.

## Wrongly accused

The original fossil find was misinterpreted by the scientists that studied it. They found the fossil of the Oviraptor near a nest containing dinosaur eggs – these eggs were assumed to belong to another dinosaur. The scientists thought the Ovirapor must have been stealing the eggs for food and so gave it its name of "egg thief."

In 1993 a team of American and Mongolian scientists found a fossil of an egg of the same kind – and this time found an Oviraptor embryo inside it. It seemed that the Oviraptor found in 1924 had been protecting its own nest!

Further evidence of the Oviraptor's "nurturing" nature came with the discovery in 1995 of a fossil Oviraptor actually sitting on its nest. The Oviraptor had its feet folded underneath its body, and a clutch of at least 15 eggs were arranged in a circle and surrounded by its forearms.

## Reproduction

A recent discovery from Jiangxi in China showed a partial skeleton of an Oviraptor who was about to give birth, with intact eggs with shells still inside the body. Examination of

the find showed that the reproductive system of an Oviraptor is something between that of reptiles and birds, having similarities to each. This is taken as further evidence of the theory that birds evolved from dinosaurs.

## Dinosaur Data

| | |
|---|---|
| PRONUNCIATION: | O-VIH-RAP-TOR |
| SUBORDER: | THERAPODA |
| FAMILY: | OVIRAPTORIDAE |
| DESCRIPTION: | BIPEDAL OMNIVORE |
| FEATURES: | TOOTHLESS BEAK, HORNY CREST IN TOP OF HEAD |
| DIET: | OMNIVOROUS |

## Tree-top grazing giant

G I A N T   P L A N T   E A T E R S

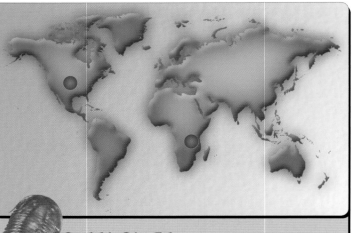

**FOSSIL FACTS**
**Fossils have been found in the USA and Africa. The first was discovered in 1900. Brachiosaurus means "arm lizard."**

Brachiosaurus was named in 1903 and gets its name from its long front limbs. It was 82 ft (25 m) long and 49 ft (15 m) high.

For many years it was thought to be the world's biggest dinosaur, but recent discoveries – such as Argentinosaurus (see page 42) – were proved to be bigger in terms of sheer mass.

## Appearance and diet

Brachiosaurus walked on four legs, and had a long neck, tiny head, and a comparatively short, thick tail. It had chisel-like teeth to nip leaves and fruit from the trees. It had nostrils on top of its head, which meant it could eat almost constantly without interfering with its breathing. It swallowed its food whole, without chewing.

To help with its digestion, Brachiosaurus swallowed stones. These stayed in its gizzard. Tough leaves and plant fibers would be ground up by the stones as they went through.

## Circulation system

To pump blood all the way up its long neck to its tiny brain, Brachiosaurus had to have a powerful heart and broad, strong blood vessels, with valves to prevent the blood obeying gravity and flowing backwards. Scientists once thought Brachiosaurus actually had two brains, the second near the hip area – but current thinking is that this was simply an enlargement in the spinal cord.

## Habitat

At first, scientists believed it must have been an aquatic dinosaur, spending all its time in the water and using its long neck and the nostrils on top of its head as a kind of snorkel for breathing. However, studies showed that water pressure would have stopped Brachiosaurus from breathing properly when submerged.

## Dinosaur Data

| | |
|---|---|
| PRONUNCIATION: | BRACK-EE-OH-SAWR-US |
| SUBORDER: | SAUROPODOMORPHA |
| FAMILY: | BRACHIOSAURIDAE |
| DESCRIPTION: | LONG-NECKED **HERBIVORE** |
| FEATURES: | HUGE FRONT LIMBS; TINY HEAD |
| DIET: | HERBIVORE |

# MEGA FACTS

- **Brachiosaurus may well have lived to be 100 years old.**

- **It probably traveled in herds.**

- **Brachiosaurus needed to consume 440 lb (200 kg) of food *every day* to fuel its massive body.**

- **It weighed 20 times as much as a large elephant!**

- **A full-size replica of a Brachiosaurus skeleton is mounted in O'Hare International Airport, Chicago.**

Scientists now believe that Brachiosaurus lived completely on land. Although their fossilized footprints have been found beside shorelines (they probably went there to drink) they have also been found in areas that 156–145 million years ago would have had very little water.

In 2003, a computer simulation run by Dr. Donald Henderson in Canada, showed that Brachiosaurus would have floated rather than sunk if it had fallen into deep water – its hollow backbones would have helped it to float, though it would probably have rolled onto its sides in the water rather than staying upright.

## Gigantic long-necked herbivore

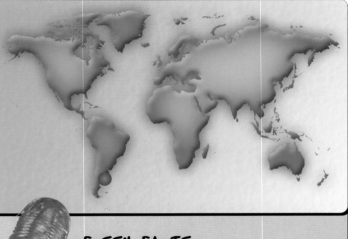

**FOSSIL FACTS**
The only fossils were found in
Argentina in 1988.

Argentinosaurus means "lizard from Argentina."
It was named in 1993 by **paleontologists**
José F. Bonaparte and Rodolfo Coria after the
country where it was found.

### Appearance

Argentinosaurus may have grown up to 130 ft (40 m) long,
69 ft (21 m) tall, and about 30 ft (9 m) wide and weighed
90–110 tons (90,000–110,000 kg).

An entire skeleton has yet to be discovered. Only about 10%
of the Argentinosaurus skeleton was found, and nothing at

all from its neck or tail. Scientists used the bones that *were*
found to work out which other dinosaurs Argentinosaurus
was related to. They then made their "best guesses" at its
appearance based on what those other dinosaurs looked like.

It would have looked very similar to a Brachiosaurus (see
page 40), with a long tail, and a tiny triangular-shaped head
on the end of its long neck. It would have needed a big,
powerful heart to pump blood all the way up that long neck
to its tiny brain.

### Backbone

Scientists think its backbone worked in a special
way to support the vast weight of the
animal. The backbones interlinked to

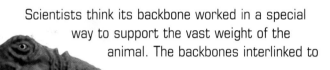

### Dinosaur Data

| | |
|---|---|
| PRONUNCIATION: | AHY-GEN-**TEEN**-OH-**SAWR**-US |
| SUBORDER: | SAUROPODOMORPHA |
| FAMILY: | TITANOSAURIA |
| DESCRIPTION: | GIGANTIC, LONG-NECKED HERBIVORE |
| FEATURES: | SPECIAL INTERLOCKING BACKBONE, LONG NECK |
| DIET: | MOSTLY CONIFERS, FLOWERS, FRUIT, AND SEEDS |

| Permian period | Triassic period | Jurassic period | Cretaceous period |
|---|---|---|---|
| 90-248 million years ago) | (248-176 million years ago) | (176-130 million years ago) | (130-66 million years ago) |

43

make the whole back into a sort of bridge of bone. Curiously for such a big animal, the bones were hollow – perhaps they evolved that way to reduce weight and let Argentinosaurus move its vast bulk around more quickly.

## Diet

Argentinosaurus was a herbivore, living on plants. It would have had to eat a huge amount to keep its massive body going, and probably spent most of its waking moments eating. Luckily, the area where it lived was full of lush vegetation. This is the area we now call Patagonia. It would have eaten mostly conifers, seeds, fruit, and flowering plants.

The biggest animal ever to live is a modern day giant, the Blue Whale. Argentinosaurus *was* the biggest animal that ever lived on land, though. Its relative, Seismosaurus was actually longer, but less tall, wide, and heavy.

Argentinosaurus reigns supreme – at least until the next "big" discovery!

# MEGA FACTS

- A single vertebra (backbone) from Argentinosaurus is taller than a child and measures 5 ft (1.5m) across!

- Argentinosarus was preyed on by the massive meat eater Giganotosaurus (see page 26) and perhaps an even larger recently discovered meat eater – *Mapusaurus Roseae*, which hunted in packs!

- Thanks to its long neck, Argentinosaurus would have no trouble looking in at a third or fourth story window.

- In its 'teenage' years when it was growing fastest, Argentinosaurus could gain about 100 lb (45 kg) a day!

- Argentinosaurus was as long as four buses!

# DIPLODOCUS

## Gigantic long-necked herbivore

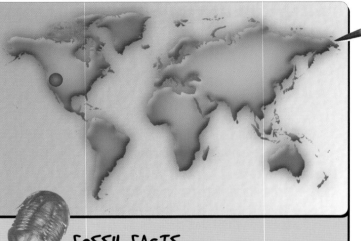

### FOSSIL FACTS
**Fossils have been found in Colorado, Montana, Utah, and Wyoming (USA). The first fossils were found at Como Bluff, Wyoming, in 1878.**

Diplodocus means "double beamed lizard." It was named in 1878, by Othniel Charles Marsh. The name comes from an unusual feature of the bones in the middle of its tail, where twin extensions of protruding bone run backward and forward. They would have protected blood vessels in the tail if it dragged on the floor, or if the dinosaur pressed its tail against the floor to help balance while rearing on its back legs.

*Diplodocus skeleton*

## Appearance

Diplodocus was one of the longest land animals that ever lived. At 89 ft (27 m) long it was a true giant. It stood around 20 ft (6 m) high at the hip and weighed 10–11 tons (10,000–11,000 kg). Diplodocus had hollow bones and so it weighed only an eighth of the similar-sized Brachiosaurus (see page 40).

Much of its length was accounted for by its long neck and even longer whip-like tail. Its head was tiny, with an elongated snout and nostril on the top of the skull.

In 1990, a new Diplodocus skeleton was found with skin impressions. This suggests Diplodocus had a row of spines down its back.

# MEGA FACTS

- The life-sized replica of diplodocus, named "Dippy", stands outside the Carnegie Museum of Natural History in Pittsburgh (USA).

- Some scientists believe Diplodocus could swing its long tail as a weapon. If so, the speed at the very tip of the tail would have broken the sound barrier!

## Brain

Diplodocus had a brain the size of a fist. It was once thought that Diplodocus had two brains, one in the skull and one close to the base of the spine. Actually, this second "brain" was simply a concentration of nerves that helped to control the back legs and tail.

Scientists believe Diplodocus could not lift its head very far from the ground. The longer neck may have allowed Diplodocus to push its neck and head a good distance into overgrown forest areas to find food. It could also swing the neck from side to side, allowing it to graze on a wide area without actually moving. Scientists think that Diplodocus would have spent almost every waking moment eating, just to keep its massive body going.

It was a **quadruped**. Each pillar-like leg had five toes, and one toe on each foot had a thumb claw, which might have been used for self-defense.

## Diet

Diplodocus was a **herbivore**. Its main food would have been conifer leaves and ferns. Its simple, peg-like teeth could strip soft foliage like ferns but couldn't chew them up. Diplodocus swallowed small stones (called gastroliths) to help grind up its food in its stomach.

### Dinosaur Data

| | |
|---|---|
| PRONUNCIATION: | DIP-LOD-OH-KUS |
| SUBORDER: | SAUROPODOMORPHA |
| FAMILY: | DILODOCIDAE |
| DESCRIPTION: | LONG-NECKED HERBIVORE |
| FEATURES: | LONG NECK, WHIPLASH TAIL, HOLLOW BONES, TINY HEAD |
| DIET: | FERNS AND CONIFERS |

# APATOSAURUS

## Formerly known as Brontosaurus

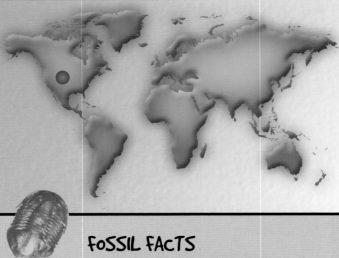

**FOSSIL FACTS**
Fossils have been found in Colorado, Oklahoma, Utah, and Wyoming, all in the USA. The first was found in 1877.

Apatosaurus means "deceptive lizard." In 1877, American **paleontologist** Othniel C. Marsh described and named a dinosaur called Apatosaurus. In 1879, he described and named another set of dinosaur remains, and – believing them to be from a different creature – christened them Brontosaurus.

## Appearance

In 1903, it was discovered that Brontosaurus was in fact simply a fully-grown Apatosaurus! However, the name Brontosaurus was not officially removed from lists until 1974, and it is still popular with many people.

Apatosaurus was some 69–90 ft (21–27 m) long, 10–15 ft (3–4.6 m) tall at the hip, and weighed 27 tons (27,000 kg). Its head was tiny at only 2 ft (60 cm) in length. Its long neck had 15 vertebrae, and a long, whip-like tail which accounted for 50 ft (15 m) of its whole length. In the front part of its jaw were peg-like teeth, ideal for stripping leaves and browsing on vegetation. Apatosaurus would have had to eat almost constantly when awake – fortunately, nostrils placed on the top of the skull meant it could eat and breathe at the same time.

Apatosaurus swallowed its food without chewing it, and to help with its digestion, it swallowed stones which stayed in its gizzard. Stones swallowed for this purpose are called gastroliths.

A study in 1999 used computer modeling to test the mobility of the neck of Apatosaurus. The results showed that they could not have lifted their heads any higher than 10–13 ft (3–4m) (just a little higher than their backs), and, most of the time, have held their heads downward or straight out. (They could move their heads freely from side to side, though.)

## Dinosaur Data

| | |
|---|---|
| PRONUNCIATION: | A-**PAT**-OH-**SAWR**-US |
| SUBORDER: | SAUROPODA |
| FAMILY: | DIPLODOCIDAE |
| DESCRIPTION: | LARGE, SLOW-MOVING HERBIVORE |
| FEATURES: | THICK LEGS, TINY HEAD, LONG NECK, LONG THIN TAIL |
| DIET: | HERBIVORE: LEAVES, PLANTS, MOSSES |

| Permian period | Triassic period | Jurassic period | Cretaceous period |
|---|---|---|---|
| (90-248 million years ago) | (248-176 million years ago) | (176-130 million years ago) | (130-66 million years ago) |

47

The biggest predator around at the time, Allosaurus (see page 72), was only 15 ft (4.6 m) tall – an Apatosaurus whose head was raised even by this limited amount would place its head 18 ft (5.4 m) off the ground, making it almost impossible for the **carnivore** to attack its head and neck.

Like other **sauropods**, Apatosaurus young hatched from huge eggs. It is assumed that Apatosaurus laid their eggs as they walked, and did not take care of their eggs.

# MEGA FACTS

- Brain the size of a large apple.

- In the 1933 film *King Kong*, an Apatosaurus was depicted as a bloodthirsty carnivore – quite unlike the gentle plant-eating giant it really was.

- Apatosaurus had thick skin to protect it. Just as well – one of its vertebrae was found with Allosaurus teeth marks in it!

- Fossilized Apatosaurus footprints have been found that measured more than 3 ft (1 m) across!

*Apatosaurus*

*Apatosaurus skeleton*

# SEISMOSAURUS

## Giant whip-tailed herbivore

Seismosaurus means "earthquake" or "earth shaker lizard", named because a creature of its fantastic size must have surely shaken the Earth as it walked. It was discovered in 1979, and described and named by David D. Gillette in 1991. Because of its huge size, and the rocks in which it was found, it took 13 years to excavate.

Seismosaurus is currently thought to be the longest animal that ever lived. Its length was estimated originally at around 170 ft (52 m) – in 2004, this was revised to 110 ft (33.5 m). This still leaves Seismosaurus at the top of the "longest dinosaur" list, and just ahead of the previous longest-ever animal, the blue whale (100 ft or 30.5 m). It probably weighed nearly 45 tons (45,000 kg).

All our information about Seismosaurus comes from the fossilized bones from the hip and part of the back, which were found in 1979. Found mingled with the fossilized bones were the fossilized remains of more than 200 "gastroliths" – small stones that Seismosaurus swallowed to help it digest its food. It is possible that the death of this specimen was caused when it swallowed a particularly large stone, which got stuck in its throat and blocked its airway.

*Seismosaurus hallorum*

*Seismosaurus*

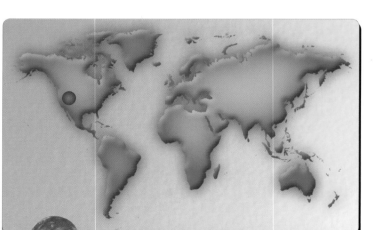

### FOSSIL FACTS
**Fossils have been found only in New Mexico, USA.**

### Appearance

Seismosaurus would have looked very like a large Diplodocus (see page 98), and may not have been much taller, as it had short legs compared to its body length. It had four pillar-like legs with five-toed feet like an elephant, a long neck, and a long, thin tail to counterbalance neck and head. Its head was tiny compared to its length, and housed a very small brain.

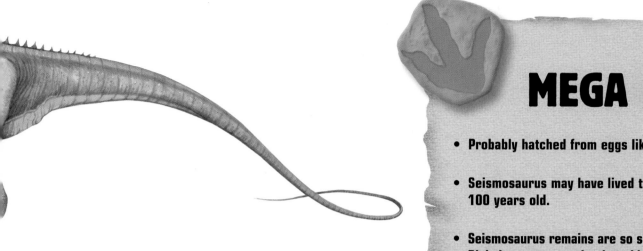

It had peg-like teeth in the front part of its mouth, ideally suited for stripping the leaves from trees and grazing on plants. It had nostrils on the top of its skull, which allowed it to eat and breathe at the same time. It may have used the whip-like tail for protection.

# MEGA FACTS

- Probably hatched from eggs like other sauropods.

- Seismosaurus may have lived to be 100 years old.

- Seismosaurus remains are so similar to those of Diplodocus, some scientists think Seismosaurus may not be a separate type of dinosaur at all, but a big new version of Diplodocus.

Seismosaurus' long neck would have usually been held parallel to the ground. It might have allowed the creature to poke its head into dense forest areas to reach leaves otherwise inaccessible to the bulky dinosaurs, or maybe to eat soft **pterodophytes** that grew in wet areas too swampy to enter safely. Its main diet item was probably conifers, huge forests of which flourished in its time.

## Dinosaur Data

| | |
|---|---|
| PRONUNCIATION: | SIZE-MOH-**SAWR**-US |
| SUBORDER: | SAUROPODOMORPHA |
| FAMILY: | DIPLODOCIDAE |
| DESCRIPTION: | INCREDIBLY LONG HERBIVORE |
| FEATURES: | LONG NECK, TINY HEAD, WHIP-LIKE TAIL |
| DIET: | LEAVES, FERNS, MOSSES |

# HADROSAURUS

## Duck-billed browsing herbivore

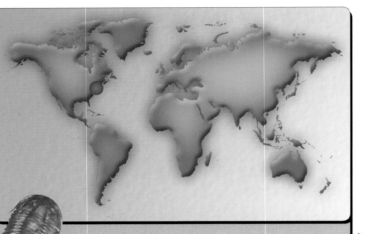

### FOSSIL FACTS
**Fossils have been found along the coast of New Jersey (USA). The first was found at Haddonfield, New Jersey, in 1858, by William Parker Foulke.**

Hadrosaurus means "heavy lizard." It was studied and named by **paleontologist** Joseph Leidy in 1858.

When Hadrosaurus was discovered, it was the most complete dinosaur skeleton that had been found. During the 1800s, various specimens of fossilized bones unlike those of any living animal, and much, much bigger, had been found in Europe and North America.

In 1841, Dr. Richard Owen, a British authority on anatomy, suggested these bones belonged to a group of large reptiles, all of which had completely died out long ago. It was he who first coined the name "dinosaurs", meaning "terrible lizards". Until Hadrosaurus came along, though, no one was able to say what one of these "dinosaurs" would have looked like.

The remains dug up in 1858 included, for the first time, enough of a dinosaur's skeleton to document its anatomy. It was also the first dinosaur fossil ever mounted and put on display in a museum. The study of dinosaurs became a well-respected science.

### Appearance and diet

Hadrosaurus was a herbivore that browsed along the shrub lands and marshes of the Atlantic coast of America 84–71 million years ago. It had a bulky body, stiff tail, and hoof-like nails on its four feet. It was a good swimmer, and may have ventured substantial distances from shore; it could also have spent time in the warm waters. It grew to between 23–30 ft (7–10 m) in length, and 10–13 ft (3–4 m) high – taller than a house if it stood on its back legs! It weighed 4,000 lb (1,900 kg).

*Hadrosaurus*

*Statue of Hadrosaurus*

# MEGA FACTS

- Even though Hadrosuarus had a whole dinosaur family named after it, no Hadrosaurus skull has ever been discovered. The shape of its head is deduced from the skulls of other duck-billed dinosaurs.

- In October 2003, a life-size statue of Hadrosaurus, cast in bronze, was unveiled in Haddonfield, close to the place the first Hadrosaurus was found.

- State Official – in 1991, Hadrosaurus became the Official "State Dinosaur" of New Jersey.

Its back legs were longer than its front legs, and this at first led scientists to believe it spent most of its time on its hind legs, in a kind of "kangaroo-like" stance. We now know that it spent most of its time on all fours. The most recent evidence suggests that Hadrosaurus held its whole rear body aloft, to balance it as it leaned its upper body forward in movements similar to those of modern birds. The front limbs would have been used for foraging.

## Dinosaur Data

| | |
|---|---|
| PRONUNCIATION: | HAD-ROW-SAWR-US |
| SUBORDER: | ORNITOPODA |
| FAMILY: | HADROSAURIDAE |
| DESCRIPTION: | MASSIVE DUCK-BILLED HERBIVORE |
| FEATURES: | BULKY BODY, TOOTHLESS BEAK |
| DIET: | LEAVES, TWIGS |

# MELANOROSAURUS

## Giant herbivorous dinosaur

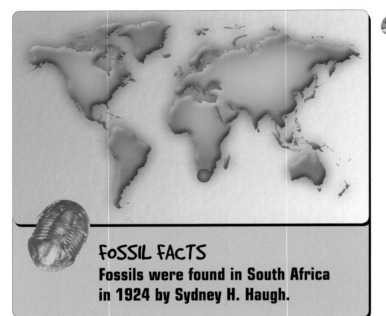

**FOSSIL FACTS**
Fossils were found in South Africa in 1924 by Sydney H. Haugh.

*Melanorosaurus*

Melanorosaurus means "Black Mountain lizard" and comes from the Greek words *melanos* (black), *oros* (mountain) and *sauros* (lizard). It was named by the British **paleontologist** Sydney H. Haugh in 1924 after the Thaba Nyama or Black Mountain in South Africa where the fossil was found.

## Appearance

Melanorosaurus lived in the early Triassic period. At 39 ft (12 m) long, 14 ft (4.3 m) tall and probably weighing around 5,000 lb (2250 kg), it was the largest land animal of its time.

Like all **sauropods**, Melanorosaurus was herbivorous and had a bulky body, long neck and tail, a relatively small skull and brain, and erect limbs reminiscent of the limbs of elephants. For some time it was believed that Melanorosaurus was a **quadruped**, as were many of the giant sauropods.

However, recently scientists have speculated that the sturdy hind limbs with their strong, dense bones could have enabled the creature to walk on its two hind legs, a theory that is given extra weight by the fact that the fore limbs were rather shorter than the hind limbs.

This ability to walk on two legs would make it a facultative **biped**, a creature that *could* walk on two legs but didn't have to – it may well have taken advantage of this ability to rear up on its hind legs in its quest for tasty leaves!

## Diet

Melanorosaurus' diet would have consisted of branches, leaves, and twigs, with its height and long neck allowing it to easily reach the tops of trees. Taking large mouthfuls of food at a time, it would use its serrated leaf-shaped teeth to snap off branches and then chew the vegetation quite effectively before swallowing. Its long neck meant it could browse over a sizable area by just moving its head and neck. This allowed it to reduce the amount of energy it would have to use up in moving – important when considering how much energy from plants it would take to maintain such a large body.

# MEGA FACTS

- Biggest dinosaur of the Triassic era! At 39 ft (12 m) long, Melanorosaurus was the largest dinosaur of its day – only in the Cretaceous period and later have larger dinosaurs been found.

- So far no Melanorosaurus skull has been discovered. However, it is believed that its skull would have been very similar in shape to those of the other giant sauropods, many of whose skulls have been found.

- While its limbs had dense bones, its spinal bones and vertebrae had hollows to reduce their weight.

## Dinosaur Data

| | |
|---|---|
| PRONUNCIATION: | MEL-UH-NOR-UH-SAWR-US |
| SUBORDER: | SAUROPODOMORPHA |
| FAMILY: | MELANOROSAURIDAE |
| DESCRIPTION: | GIANT LONG-NECKED HERBIVORE |
| FEATURES: | LONG NECK AND TAIL, BULKY BODY, LEAF-SHAPED SERRATED TEETH |
| DIET: | BRANCHES, LEAVES, AND TWIGS |

53

# TITANOSAURUS

## Giant armored herbivore

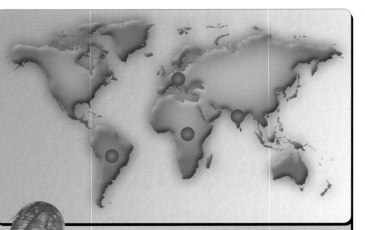

**FOSSIL FACTS**
Fossils have been found in Europe, India, Africa, and South America. The first fossils were discovered in India.

### Appearance

Titanosaurus had a bulky body, a long "whiplash" tail, and a tiny head on the end of its long neck. The head was incredibly small compared to the rest of its body, but was quite wide. It had large nostrils, and its nasal bones formed a sort of raised crest on its skull. It had very small teeth.

It grew to around 39–59 ft (12–18 m) in length and about 10–16 ft (3–5 m) tall at the hips. It would have weighed about 15 tons (14,700 kg).

This dinosaur walked on all fours. Its front legs were stout and stocky. Its back legs were longer than the front ones, and Titanosaurus would have been able to rear up onto these strong back legs to reach higher up trees for food. It had a very flexible spine, making rearing up easy.

Titanosaurus means "titanic lizard." The dinosaur was named by Richard Lydekker in 1877 – almost 20 years after its remains were first discovered.

Titanosaurus was a **sauropod** dinosaur, like Argentinosaurus (see page 42) and Brachiosaurus (see page 40).

## Dinosaur Data

| | |
|---|---|
| PRONUNCIATION: | TIE-TAN-OH-SAWR-US |
| SUBORDER: | SAUROPODA |
| FAMILY: | TITANOSAURIDAE |
| DESCRIPTION: | GIANT ARMORED HERBIVORE |
| FEATURES: | LONG NECK, FLEXIBLE BACK, ARMORED SKIN |
| DIET: | CONIFERS, PALMS, GRASSES |

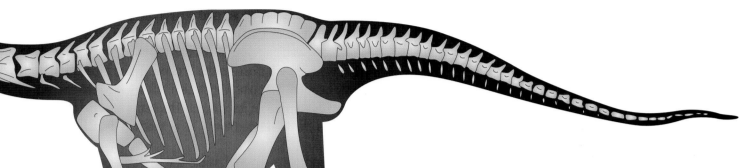

Titanosaurus had a very wide chest, which placed its legs and feet widely apart. Scientists have discovered fossilized footprints (we call these "fossilized trackways") showing that Titanosaurus tracks are much wider than those of other sauropod dinosaurs.

Fossilized impressions of Titanosaurus' skin have survived, so we know that it had armor to protect it. Its skin was covered with a pattern of small "bead-like" scales surrounding larger scales.

## Diet

The fossilized remains of Titanosaur dung show that Titanosaurus had quite a broad diet. It ate pretty much any plant material – remains from conifer twigs and leaves, palms, and grasses were all found. Titanosaurus lived in herds, browsing from place to place to find fresh vegetation to eat.

## Reproduction

Titanosaurus laid eggs, and the whole herd probably shared one large nesting ground, where they dug nests and then buried their eggs under dirt and vegetation. Their eggs would have measured only 4–5 in. (11–12 cm) across.

## Latest discoveries

In May 2006, Italian scientists announced the discovery of four well-preserved Titanosaur skeletons in South America. There are skeletons of young Titanosaurs as well as adults.

# MEGA FACTS

- Although Titanosaurus eggs were only about 5 in. (12 cm) across, the babies that hatched would grow to be longer than a bus!

- Living in herds would have given Titanosaurus protection against large predators.

55

# STEGOSAURUS

## Ridge-backed slow-moving herbivore

**FOSSIL FACTS**
Fossils have been found in the western USA, western Europe, southern India, China, and southern Africa.

Stegosaurus was named by Othniel Marsh in 1877. Its name means "roofed lizard." It was named after the double row of alternating bony plates embedded in its back (it had 17 plates altogether).

### Appearance

Stegosaurus was big, heavy, and slow-moving. It grew to between 30–40 ft (9–12 m) long and up to 13 ft (4 m) high. It weighed in at up to 3 tons (3,000 kg).

Its back legs were longer and straighter than its front legs, which stuck out somewhat to the sides. This gave it a downward-sloping shape toward its small, pointed head. Its head was carried close to the ground. It had a toothless, horny beak for cropping vegetation, with small leaf-shaped teeth further back in its cheeks. The back feet had three toes, while the front feet had five – all of them had hoof-like claws.

At the end of its short, flexible tail, Stegosaurus had 3 ft (1 m) spikes, which we now know stuck out sideways rather than upwards. The tail was held horizontal to the ground and could be swung upwards and sideways as a weapon, to defend against predatory dinosaurs.

| Permian period (90-248 million years ago) | Triassic period (248-176 million years ago) | Jurassic period (176-130 million years ago) | Cretaceous period (130-66 million years ago) |

## Armored plates

In addition to its back plates, in 1992 it was discovered that Stegosaurus had chainmail-like armored plates protecting its throat and hip areas.

The pointy back plates were originally assumed to be armor, for defence against predators. Then it was discovered that they were rather fragile, and not ideally placed for protection. It has been suggested that they may have served only display purposes, such as distinguishing between the male and female of the species – but both male and female Stegosaurus had them.

For a long time, the most popular theory was that the plates were used for regulating body temperature. The most recent theory suggests that the plates were simply used by members of the species to recognise others of their own kind.

Stegosaurus lived in family groups, possibly even in herds. Stegosaurus was not only the largest, but one of the last of the **stegosaurs**. Towards the end of the Jurassic period, a minor mass extinction occurred, and most of the stegosaurs died out.

### Dinosaur Data

| | |
|---|---|
| PRONUNCIATION: | STEG-OH-SAWR-US |
| SUBORDER: | THRYREOPHORA |
| FAMILY: | STEGOSAURIDAE |
| DESCRIPTION: | SLOW-MOVING, HEAVY HERBIVORE |
| FEATURES: | SPINES ON BACK, HEAVY SPIKED TAIL |
| DIET: | LOW-GROWING LEAVES AND PLANTS |

# MEGA FACTS

- Stegosaurus was nearly as big as a bus – but its brain was only the size of a table-tennis ball, weighing a tiny 2.4 oz (71 g).

- The most complete Stegosaurus found was discovered in Colorado in 1992. Its excavators gave it the highly-suitable nickname of "Spike."

- Under its feet, Stegosaurus had pads of spongy tissue to help cushion its weight.

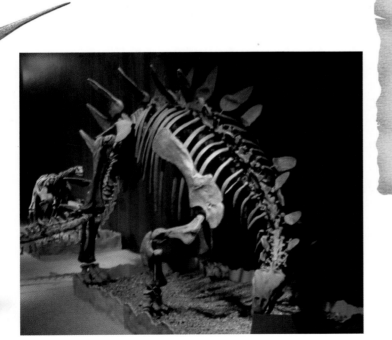

*Stegosaurus skeleton*

# ANKYLOSAURUS

## Tank-like armored herbivore

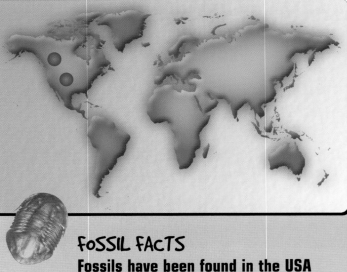

**FOSSIL FACTS**
Fossils have been found in the USA and Canada. The first specimen was found in 1906.

Ankylosaurus means "crooked lizard" or "fused lizard" – the name refers to the fusion of many of its bones to provide extra protection. It was named in 1908.

### Appearance

Ankylosaurus was the biggest of the armored dinosaurs. It died out in the **K-T extinction event** 65 million years ago. Its armor was impressive – back, sides, and tail completely protected.

Even its eyelids had plates of bone. In addition to their armor, they had rows of bony spikes that projected from their flanks and bony knobs on its back.

Its body was low-slung, and very wide. It moved slowly on four solid legs, and the back legs were longer than the front ones. Its rather triangular skull was massive.

Four "horns" stuck out from the back side of the skull, giving extra protection. The skull was also very thick, leaving room for only a small brain. It had a wide muzzle, and a toothless beak of a mouth for grazing. Farther back in its mouth were leaf-shaped cheek teeth for grinding up vegetation.

### Tail

Ankylosaurus' tail ended in a thick bony "club", which was supported by the last few vertebrae in the tail, which were fused together to support it. Attached to these vertebrae were thick tendons, enabling the "club" to be swung with sufficient force to break bones.

Ankylosaurus skeleton

# MEGA FACTS

- In 1996, Ankylosaur trackways (fossilized footprints) were found in Brazil. Speed estimates made using the pattern of these prints revealed that Ankylosaurus could move "at a decent jog" when needed.

- Ankylosaurus would have had a huge gut, probably with a fermentation chamber to help digest the tough plant material, which would have produced impressive amounts of gas!

would criss cross from layer to layer. (The pattern of these fibers can still be seen in fossils after millions of years.) This would give the plate great strength in all directions. These "composite" dinosaur plates were thinner and lighter than the simpler but weaker ones possessed by other species of armored dinosaur. Layers of them could withstand great amounts of stress – for example, when the Ankylosaurus swung its tail hard in defense.

As a last resort, it could swing the club like a weapon to defend itself. It also probably dropped flat to the ground if attacked, protecting its vulnerable stomach and leaving only its heavily armored areas available to its attacker.

## Armor structure

In 2004, a study showed that Ankylosaurus' armor had a complex structure, with collagen fibers interwoven in the bone calcium of the plates, forming mats that

### Dinosaur Data

| | |
|---|---|
| PRONUNCIATION: | ANG-KI-LO-SAWR-US |
| SUBORDER: | THYREOPHORA |
| FAMILY: | ANKYLOSAURIDAE |
| DESCRIPTION: | ARMOR-PLATED HERBIVORE |
| FEATURES: | CLUB-LIKE TAIL; HEAVILY ARMORED BACK AND SIDES |
| DIET: | LOW-LYING PLANTS |

59

# KENTROSAURUS

## Slow and spiky herbivore

### FOSSIL FACTS
Fossils have been found in Tendaguru, in Tanzania (Africa). The first fossils were discovered by a German expedition in 1909–1912.

### Dinosaur Data

| | |
|---|---|
| PRONUNCIATION: | KEN-TROH-SAWR-US |
| FAMILY: | STEGOSAURIDAE |
| DESCRIPTION: | PLATED AND SPIKED HERBIVORE |
| FEATURES: | ROW OF LONG SHARP SPIKES DOWN BACK AND TAIL |
| DIET: | FERNS, LOW-GROWING RIVERSIDE PLANTS |

Kentrosaurus means "spiked lizard" or "pointed lizard." It was first described and named by Edwin Hennig in 1915.

### Appearance

It is named after the dramatic double row of bony spikes that ran from halfway down its back to the end of its tail, standing almost upright in a zigzag arrangement. Each spike was around 12 in. (30 cm) high. At the end of its strong, thick tail it had two pairs of sharp spikes, each nearly 3 ft (1 m) long. It would defend itself against predators by swinging its tail like a weapon.

Above the row of spikes, it had nine pairs of small bony plates sticking up along its upper back, shoulders, and neck. These plates contained blood vessels. They were too small to help it regulate its body temperature (as other dinosaurs with larger back plates may have done) but may have been used for display

as well as defense. If used for display, they were probably brightly colored.

It grew between 8 ft (2.5 m) and 16 ft (5 m) in length. Its height was around 6 ft (1.8 m), and it carried its long, powerful tail higher than its head, which was held low to the ground.

| Permian period (90-248 million years ago) | Triassic period (248-176 million years ago) | Jurassic period (176-130 million years ago) | Cretaceous period (130-66 million years ago) |

## Diet

It had a tiny, narrow head ending in a toothless beak. Small teeth farther back in its cheeks helped it to mash up the ferns and lush riverside plants that it grazed on. The area where Kentrosaurus fossils were discovered would have been close to a large river 156–150 million years ago when Kentrosaurus lived. Scientists believe it would have grazed the riverbanks for its food.

Its back legs were twice as long as its front legs, and it may have been able to stand up for short periods of time on just its back legs, to reach higher-up vegetation such as leaves.

There is strong evidence that Kentrosaurus moved and lived in herds.

# MEGA FACTS

- Kentrosaurus was once believed to have two brains! Scientists now know that this second brain was merely a nerve cluster, which controlled the tail and hind legs.

- An almost-complete Kentrosaurus skeleton (one of the only two ever found) at one time stood in the Humboldt Museum at the University of Berlin. During World War II, the museum was bombed and practically all the bones lost.

- Its olfactory bulbs (the area of the brain controlling smell) were very well developed, so it had a keen sense of smell.

# EDMONTONIA

## Spiny armored herbivore

ARMORED DINOSAURS

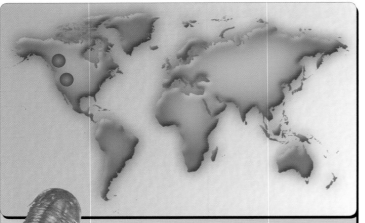

FOSSIL FACTS
Fossils have been found in Alberta (Canada) and Montana, South Dakota, and Texas (all in the USA). The first specimen was found by George Paterson in 1924.

Edmontonia means "from Edmonton." It was named in 1928 by C. M. Sternberg, and its name comes from where it was found – close to the Edmonton rock formation in Alberta (Canada).

It was an **ankylosaur**, one of a group of armored **herbivores** that lived 76–68 million years ago. There were three main goups of ankylosaurs – ankylosaurids (like Ankylosaurus, polacanthids, and nodosaurids. Edmontonia was a nodosaurid.

Edmontonia was one of the largest nodosaurids at 20–23 ft (6–7 m) in length. It weighed in at around 3.5 tons

(3,000 kg), and its bulky body was supported on four stocky legs. It grew to around 6 ft (2 m) high, and could flatten itself to the ground if attacked to protect its soft underbelly. Even its stiff tail was armored!

It had **scutes** (bony plates) on its back and head, sharp spikes along its back and tail. Four large spikes stuck out from its shoulders on each side. Small cheek teeth further back in its weak jaws helped it grind up vegetation before swallowing it. The head was probably covered in armored scales to protect the brain, and two collars of flat bony plates protected the back of the neck – smaller bands of plates continued down to the armored tail.

# MEGA FACTS

- Edmontonia had specially arranged shoulder muscles that let it draw in its front legs if attacked and hold their body close to the ground.

- The large spikes that stuck out from its shoulders were most likely used in contests of strength with others of its own kind.

- Edmontonia had very wide feet, which they would have needed in the mostly low-lying coastal areas they inhabited to walk safely on wet and marshy ground.

- Slow-moving Edmontonia would have needed every bit of its impressive armor, as it shared time and territory with Tyrannosaurus Rex!

## Dinosaur Data

| | |
|---|---|
| PRONUNCIATION: | ED-MON-**TONE**-EE-AH |
| SUBORDER: | THYREOPHORA |
| FAMILY: | NODOSAURIDAE |
| DESCRIPTION: | TANK-LIKE HERBIVORE |
| FEATURES: | BONY PLATES AND SPIKES FOR PROTECTION |
| DIET: | LOW-LYING PLANTS |

# SCELIDOSAURUS

## Ponderous armored plant eater

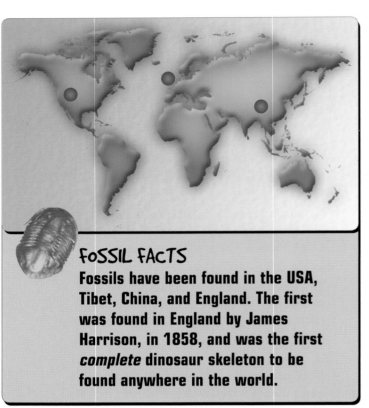

Scelidosaurus means "limb lizard." It was named by Sir Richard Owen in 1859. It lived around 206–200 million years ago.

*Scelidosaurus*

## Appearance

The bony plates in its skin give Scelidosaurus a distinct resemblance to the later **ankylosaurs**. However, the bony plates down its back, and the heavy body raised at the hips also give it similarities to another later dinosaur, Stegosaurus (see page 56). Scientists believe both **ankylosaurs** and **stegosaurs** may be descended from Scelidosaurus. Its brain was very small compared to its body size, indicating low intelligence.

ARMORED DINOSAURS

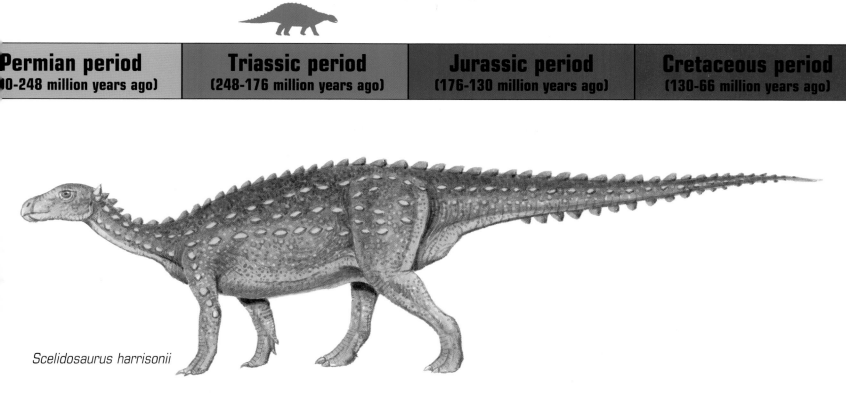

*Scelidosaurus harrisonii*

Scelidosaurus was a low-slung plant eater, with a small head, stocky legs, and a long, stiffened tail. Its neck was quite long compared to other armored dinosaurs. It weighed some 200–250 lb (440–550 kg) and grew to 5 ft (1.5 m) tall. It was around 13 ft (4 m) long.

It moved slowly, grazing almost constantly on low-growing soft-leaved plants, flowers, and fruits. Its narrow beak contained small leaf-shaped teeth in the front of the upper jaw, useful for slicing flowers and fruits off plants rather than for chewing food. It *could* chew, but only with a very simple up and down movement of its jaws.

## Defense

The **scutes** that protected it had pointy "studs" on them, and small three-pronged horns stuck out from behind its ears. If attacked, it would have crouched low to the ground, hiding its soft underbelly and leaving its attacker to fruitlessly bite at its armored back, flanks and tail.

We know very little for certain about what it ate or where precisely it made its home, as the fossilized remains have

so far all been found away from the creature's natural habitat – the bodies had been washed out to sea after the animal died. They were not marine creatures or amphibians, but probably lived on riverbanks. Perhaps some of them were drowned when the river overflowed, and washed out to sea to be buried and preserved.

### Dinosaur Data

| | |
|---|---|
| PRONUNCIATION: | SKEL-EE-DOH-**SAWR**-US |
| SUBORDER: | THYREOPHORA |
| FAMILY: | SCELIDOSAURIDAE |
| DESCRIPTION: | ARMORED HERBIVORE |
| FEATURES: | BONY ARMOR PLATES AND SPIKES |
| DIET: | LOW-GROWING PLANTS |

## MEGA FACTS

- It is thought Scelidosaurus might well have been an ancestor of both Ankylosaurus and Stegosaurus.

- Scelidosaurus has been classified at different times as a stegosaur or an ankylosaur. Scientists still do not wholly agree about which group it belongs to.

- Although it usually walked on all four legs, some scientists think that Scelidosaurus' strong hind legs and long tail may have allowed it to run on just its back legs for short distances.

- Young Scelidosaurus may have added extra protein to their diet by eating insects.

# SCUTELLOSAURUS

## Tiny armored herbivore

FOSSIL FACTS

**Fossils have been found in Arizona, North America.**

Scutellosaurus means "little shield lizard." It gets its name from the bony armor "shields" called **scutes** that covered its tiny body. It was named by Edwin Colbert in 1981. We know this little dinosaur from the remains of two incomplete skeletons and hundreds of bony armor plates that have been found in Arizona (USA).

## Appearance

Scutellosaurus was a primitive dinosaur. It is the oldest known armored dinosaur, and is thought to be related to **Lesothaurus**. When we think of dinosaurs we tend to think of massive creatures, but Scutellosaurus was no bigger than a dog – 4 ft (1.2 m) long, 5 ft (1.5 m) tall at the hips, and weighing around 22 lb (10 kg). Its long thin tail accounted for much of its length, being twice the length of its combined body and head.

Its thin hind legs were much longer than its forelimbs – scientists believe it probably walked most of the time (and rested) on four legs, but if attacked could rise up onto its back legs and run away at decent speed, its long tail helping to balance it. A creature that can walk on both two and four legs is said to be **semi-bipedal**. Its own ancestors had been fully bipedal – its descendants would be **quadrupeds**.

## Scutes

More than 300 bony scutes protected this little creature, running along its back and tail. Six different types of the bony plates have been found. The largest may have formed one or two rows down the center of its back.

## Diet

Scutellosaurus was a **herbivore**, and spent much of its time grazing, using its simple cheek teeth to crush and slice soft and fleshy low-growing vegetation. Its jaw was particularly well adapted for cropping leafy plants.

## Dinosaur Data

| | |
|---|---|
| PRONUNCIATION: | SKU-**TEL**-OH-**SAWR**-US |
| SUBORDER: | THYREOPHORA |
| DESCRIPTION: | TINY ARMORED HERBIVORE |
| FEATURES: | LONG THIN TAIL, ARMORED PLATES |
| DIET: | PLANTS, SEEDS, FRUITS |

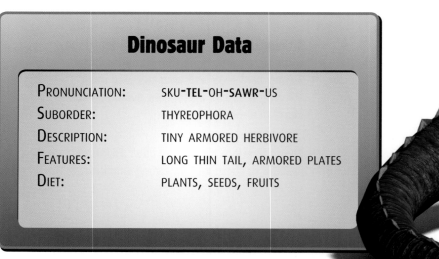

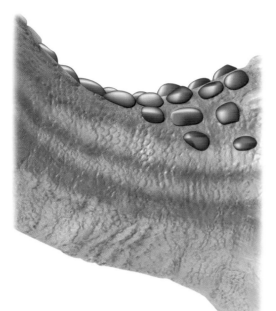

## Descendants

Scutellossaurus is most likely an ancestor of the later large armored **ankylosaurs** and **stegosaurs**. Many scientists think that as it developed heavier armored plates – especially in the head and neck region – its body would have become heavier and heavier at the front, eventually forcing it to walk on all fours permanently and paving the way for its larger quadrupedal descendants.

# MEGA FACTS

- Scutellosaurus had two ways to defend itself against attack – it was protected by its armored skin, and it could rise up onto its back legs to run away.

- Any predator trying to take a bite out of this little guy was in for a shock – its skin was protected by more than 300 armor plates!

- Scutellosaurus had a short skull. Its tail, on the other hand, was twice the length of its body and head put together.

# MINMI

## Small and unusual armored herbivore

This dinosaur was named and described by Ralph Molnar in 1980. It was named after the place where the first pieces of its fossil remains had been found, Minmi Crossing.

Minmi was the first armored dinosaur found south of the equator. It is also the most complete dinosaur skeleton ever found in Australia.

### Appearance

Minmi seems to have been a very primitive **ankylosaur,** and scientists have found it hard to classify. It has features in common with both ankylosaurs and **nodosaurs**, but is not identical to either. Its snout arched higher than the rest of its skull, which is common in nodosaurs. It had armored plates like an ankylosaur's – but its legs were longer, and it had no "club" at the end of its tail.

It would have been about the size of a year-old calf, growing to only 6–10 ft (2–3 m) long and about 3 ft (1 m) high, and weighing around 3,740 lb (1,700 kg). Its back legs were longer than its front ones, and it went on all fours. Minmi would have lived on the low-growing plants of the floodplains and woodlands where it roamed.

As well as having longer legs than ankylosaurus, Minmi had extra bony plates added to its backbone. These strengthened its back, helping support the weight of its armor. Extra muscles attached to these extra plates could have allowed Minmi to run at reasonable speed.

### Defense

Minmi had skin armored with large bony plates (called **scutes**) and smaller pea-sized bones (called **ossicles**) embedded all over it. Even Minmi's underbelly was protected by small bony plates, which makes it unique among the whole thyreophoran suborder of dinosaurs.

Apart from this armor, Minmi had no real way to defend itself – it lacked the tail 'club' possessed by most ankylosaurs. Running away was probably its best defense!

Minmi was the only ankylosaur to have **paravertebrae**. Some scientists have suggested that these are actually **tendons** which have ossified (changed into bone) rather than true bones.

### FOSSIL FACTS
**Fossils have been found in Queensland, Australia. The first fossils were discovered by Alan Batholomai near Roma, Queensland, in 1964.**

*Minmi skeleton*

Minmi has much in common with both ankylosaurs and nodosaurs, but it may turn out to be a wholly new type of armored dinosaur!

# MEGA FACTS

• In 1990 an almost-complete Minmi skeleton was found in Queensland. It was so well preserved that wrinkles in its skin could be made out from the pattern of the ossicles.

• Minmi has the shortest name ever given to a dinosaur.

• Recent studies have been able to analyze the contents of a Minmi stomach. It was able to chew its food into smaller pieces before swallowing them.

## Dinosaur Data

| | |
| --- | --- |
| PRONUNCIATION: | MIN-MEE |
| SUBORDER: | THYREOPHORA |
| DESCRIPTION: | SMALL ARMORED HERBIVORE |
| FEATURES: | ARMORED PLATES ON BELLY |
| DIET: | LOW-GROWING SOFT PANTS MATERIALS, LEAVES, FRUIT, STEMS |

# COLD-BLOODED CREATURES

People disagree over whether dinosaurs were cold-blooded or warm-blooded. It used to be assumed that dinosaurs were cold-blooded like their reptile ancestors. But some **paleontologists** have recently argued that at least some dinosaurs were fast, active, competed against hot-blooded mammals, lived in cool areas, were related to birds, and therefore were warm-blooded.

## Cold-blooded creatures

Cold-blooded animals, like lizards and snakes, control their body temperature by their behavior, moving in and out of the sun during the day. This is called the ectothermic ('outside heat') method.

## Warm-blooded creatures

Warm-blooded animals (birds and mammals) convert food energy into body heat, the endothermic ('inside heat') method.

*Alligator*

To cool off, endothermic animals sweat, pant, wallow in water, or flap their ears to cool the blood.

70

*Thescelosaurus*

## Heat control in dinosaurs

Some dinosaurs seem to have had heat controlling structures on their bodies. For example, Spinosaurus and Ouranosaurus had large sails on their backs, and Stegosaurus had numerous plates. These devices were probably used for the collection and removal of heat. This suggests that they needed these structures to control their body temperature and that they were cold-blooded.

## Circulation systems

Laellynasaura was a small but extraordinary dinosaur that lived in dense polar forests near the South Pole during the early Cretaceous period. The amazing aspect of its life was that it lived inside the Antarctic Circle, and was too small

*Laellynasaura*

to migrate north during the winter. This meant that it would have had to survive several months of continual darkness and subzero temperatures – conditions that would not favor a small, cold-blooded dinosaur.

The huge dinosaurs and the tiny dinosaurs might have used different heat-regulation strategies, just as they used different strategies for other aspect of living.

Many of the big dinosaurs, such as Tyrannosaurus Rex (see page 24) and Iguanodon (see page 86), held their heads high above their bodies. To pump blood up to their brains would have required high pressure, far higher than the delicate blood vessels in their lungs could withstand. Warm-blooded animals deal with this problem by having two blood circuits and internally divided hearts. Some scientists suggest that large dinosaurs would also have needed a divided heart and must therefore be warm-blooded.

However, while it is true that some dinosaurs must have had a divided heart to get blood to their heads, they did not necessarily need to be warm-blooded for this. Perhaps they were a combination of having a warm-blooded heart and lung system, with cold-blooded ways to control temperature. Modern alligators are an example of this, as they have a functionally divided heart but are still cold-blooded.

In 2000 the fossil of a Thescelosaurus was found to have a mammal-like, four-chambered heart. Until then dinosaurs were thought to have had only three-chambered hearts. This suggests not only that Thescelosaurus may have been warm-blooded, but that many other dinosaurs may have been warm-blooded as well.

# TRICERATOPS

## Gigantic three-horned herbivore

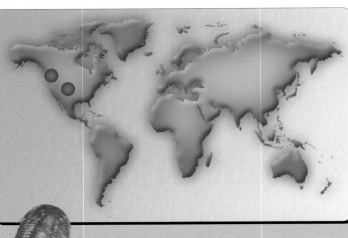

### FOSSIL FACTS
Fossils have been found in North America and Canada. The first fossils were found in 1888.

### Dinosaur Data

| | |
|---|---|
| PRONUNCIATION: | TRY-**SER**-A-TOPS |
| SUBORDER: | MARGINOCEPHALIA (FRINGED HEADS) |
| FAMILY: | CERATOPSIDAE |
| DESCRIPTION: | HUGE PLODDING HERBIVORE |
| FEATURES: | HUGE HEAVY SKULL, THREE HORNS, AND BONY NECK FRILL |
| DIET: | PLANTS AND SHRUBS |

The name Triceratops means "three-horned face" and was chosen because of the creature's most noticeable feature – the three horns on its head. It was fully named *triceratops horridus* ("horrible three-horned face").

## Horns and frill

The three horns are striking – one on its snout, and a pair above the eyes about 3 ft (1 m) long. Its other distinctive feature is the bony, stud-surrounded 'frill' at the back of its skull. Scientists have suggested various functions for this frill, but have yet to decide on one. All the following uses have been suggested:

- battling rival Triceratops for status, territory, or food
- display (for communication or attracting mates)
- anchor points for the mighty jaw muscles
- body temperature regulation (by adding to the creature's body surface area and so making absorbing heat, or cooling off, easier)
- protection against **carnivores** biting its neck and front part of body.

Triceratops was a member of the **ceratopsian** dinosaur family – large, horned dinosaurs that lived in herds. They were one of the latest dinosaur families to evolve.

## Appearance

Triceratops grew to around 29 ft (9 m) long and 10 ft (3 m) tall, and weighed in at around 12,100 lb (5,500 kg). It had a sharp, parrot-shaped beak that allowed it to break up very tough vegetation, which

# MEGA FACTS

- It has been estimated that Triceratops could have run at some 15 mph (24 km/h), even on its short legs – helpful, since it could not take long strides to flee from carnivores such as Tyrannosaurus Rex (see page 24)! Even this didn't always help – several Triceratops skeletons show bite marks that match the teeth of Tyrannosaurus Rex.

- As well as using its sharp beak to slice up vegetation, Triceratops probably also used it in self-defense.

- Triceratops had one of the largest skulls of any land animal so far discovered, sometimes 10 ft (3 m) in length.

- Triceratops is the official state dinosaur of Wyoming and the official state fossil of South Dakota

was then pushed further back into its shearing cheek teeth. It had sturdy short legs and went on all fours. Its head was large, almost a third the length of its barrel-shaped body at 6-9 ft (2–3 m).

Fossilized teeth from Triceratops are among the most commonly found fossils in western North America, and over 50 skulls have been found. Scientists believe it was the dominant herbivore in that area about 72–65 million years ago.

73

# PROTOCERATOPS

## Small, hook-beaked herbivore

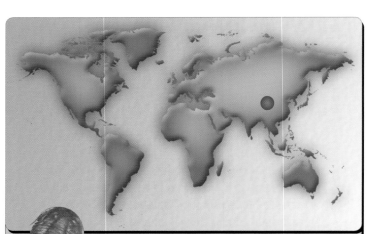

**FOSSIL FACTS**
**Fossils have been found in Asia. The first remains were found by Roy Chapman Andrews, in the Gobi Desert, Mongolia, in 1922.**

Protoceratops was small. It grew to about 6 ft (2 m) in length and 30 in. (75 cm) high, but weighed some 880 lb (400 kg). Its skeleton was made of strong, thick bone. It had four short legs, with broad, clawed feet that may have allowed it to run for a short time if threatened. It may even have been able to briefly stand on its hind legs. Most of the time, however, it would have moved slowly and ponderously on all fours.

Its mouth was a strong, curved, parrot-shaped beak, with the upper jaw being longer than the lower. It would have allowed Protoceratops to slice and cut tough plants and vegetation and then push these further back into its jaws, where it could chew them up with the teeth in its cheeks.

Protoceratops means "first horned face" or "earliest horned face." It was named by Walter Granger and W. K. Gregory. It is sometimes also referred to by the shorter name of "ceratops."

## Appearance

Protoceratops was one of the earliest members of the *ceratopsian* family, and may have been the ancestor of the later horned dinosaurs like Triceratops (see page 72). It lacked well-developed horns and had instead a thick "bump" of bone on its snout, and small bumps above its eyes — exactly where later horned dinosaurs would have their horns. It also had a large neck frill at the back of its skull.

## Skull and frill

The skull of Protoceratops was especially massive, and special muscles were probably attached to its bony neck frill to help it hold up its heavy head. The skull of a Protoceratops made up nearly half of its whole body length!

Its broad, bony neck frill grew as the Protoceratops aged. Scientists have suggested various functions for this frill – to protect the neck, to impress other Protoceratops, or to

anchor jaw muscles. Some believe it may have been brightly colored to help the Protoceratops attract a mate or to intimidate enemies. Like modern day zebras, Protoceratops probably lived in herds.

### Dinosaur Data

| | |
|---|---|
| PRONUNCIATION: | PRO-TOE-**SERR**-A-TOPS |
| SUBORDER: | MARGINOCEPHALIA |
| FAMILY: | PROTOCERATOPSIDAE |
| DESCRIPTION: | SMALL, HEAVY, HUGE-SKULLED HERBIVORE |
| FEATURES: | MASSIVE SKULL, NECK FRILL |
| DIET: | TOUGH PLANTS AND VEGETATION |

## MEGA FACTS

- A robotic protoceratops has been created at the Massachusetts Institute of Technology.

- In 1971, the fossil remains of a Velociraptor locked in combat with a Protoceratops were found in Mongolia.

## Tiny bipedal herbivore

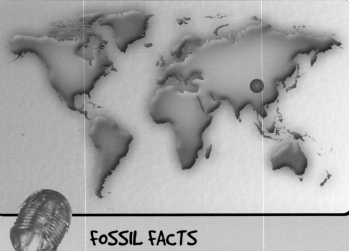

FOSSIL FACTS
**Fossils have been found in Mongolia, China.**

Some scientists believe the neck frill may have been brightly colored, to help the dinosaur attract a mate or to intimidate enemies. It seems unlikely that little Microceratops did much intimidating. Running away would be its best defense.

Its limbs were particularly slender compared to those of other dinosaurs. Its hind legs were longer than its front ones, and scientists believe it would have been able to stand up on its hind legs to run and move around (it would have been **bipedal**), though it may have gone down on all fours to graze and browse for food.

The lower part of its hind legs was much longer than the upper part, suggesting Microceratops would have been a swift runner. The front legs, or 'arms', really were tiny in comparison – a bone from the upper part of a Microceratops front limb was only 4 in. (10 cm) long.

Microceratops means "tiny horned face." It was named in 1953 and is the smallest known horned dinosaur.

This tiny, slender herbivore lived in Asia, around 80 million years ago. It was a **cerotopsian** and became extinct at the end of the Cretaceous period.

## Appearance

Small and slim, Microceratops was almost fragile-looking, with a small body and slender limbs. It was closely related to the larger Protoceratops and looked a lot like its bigger relative.

It grew to a mere 30 in. (76 cm) long and 24 in. (60 cm) high. This was a dinosaur you could have picked up in one hand.

Its head was around 8 in. (20 cm) long, and it had a horny parrot-like beak. A small bony neck frill jutted from the back of its skull. Despite its name, it lacked any real horns. Scientists have suggested various functions for the neck frill (all the ceratopsian dinosaurs had one) – it might have been to protect the neck, to impress other Microceratops, or to anchor jaw muscles.

## Diet

Microceratops was an herbivore that spent much of its time eating. It fed on **ferns**, **cycads,** and **conifers**, using its sharp parrot-like beak to bite off leaves and needles. These would then be pushed back farther into its mouth where cheek teeth could grind up the food before it was swallowed.

Microceratops probably lived in herds, grazing from place to place. It laid eggs, and the herd most likely shared one big nesting area, as a defense against larger predators.

# MEGA FACTS

- Microceratops appeared as part of the herd in the Walt Disney film *Dinosaur* (2000).

- Microceratops was not quite the smallest dinosaur that ever lived – that was *Compsognathus Longpipes*, which was only the size of a chicken.

## Dinosaur Data

| | |
|---|---|
| PRONUNCIATION: | MY-KRO-**SAYR**-AH-TOPS |
| SUBORDER: | MARGINOCEPHALIA |
| FAMILY: | PROTOCERATOPSIDAE |
| DESCRIPTION: | TINY FRILLED HERBIVORE |
| FEATURES: | SMALL SIZE, LONG HIND LEGS, FRILL |
| DIET: | FERNS, CYCADS, CONIFERS |

# LEPTOCERATOPS

## Small and swift parrot-beaked herbivore

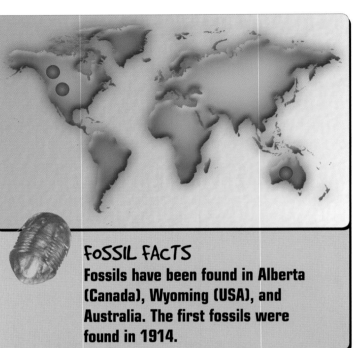

### FOSSIL FACTS
**Fossils have been found in Alberta (Canada), Wyoming (USA), and Australia. The first fossils were found in 1914.**

Leptoceratops grew to around 8 ft (2.4 m) long. Scientists believe it may have spent most of its time walking or standing on its back legs. Its forelimbs had five-fingered hands with claws that could be used for grasping vegetation. It would still have been capable of moving on all fours. Some scientists even think it may have used its powerful back legs to dig burrows in which to hide from predators.

In 1999, remains from six different Leptoceratops were found close together in a **bonebed**, suggesting that perhaps they spent at least some time in social groups.

This small, agile **ceratopsian** dinosaur was described in 1914, and named by Barnum Brown in the same year. No complete skeleton for it has been discovered – we know it from five skulls and varied skeletal remains.

## Appearance

A recent study has suggested that Leptoceratops had an extended beak taking up much of its face. Leptoceratops had only a few teeth, farther back in its jaws, which are different to those of other ceratopsians in that, instead of having double roots, its teeth had a single root per tooth. This may have meant they were less firmly anchored in its jaw – a potential problem when feeding on tough vegetation. It could use its sharp, parrot-shaped beak to slice off leaves, or needles, and to break open fruits and seeds.

Leptoceratops lacked horns, but did have a neck frill where the bones at the back of its skull formed a peak – this frill was small and flat, but distinctive.

Leptoceratops is believed to have been one of the fastest ceratopsians – perhaps even *the* fastest.

# MEGA FACTS

- Leptocaratops was, until very recently, believed to have lived only in North America and Canada, where almost all fossil remains of it have been found. More recently, fossilized Leptoceratops bones have been found in Australia, showing that this primitive herbivore may have lived all over the world.

- The fossil finds in Australia also date from the early Cretaceous period, whereas all previous finds dated from the end of that period. It seems Leptoceratops may have walked the Earth for some 50 million years!

- Leptoceratops' teeth were different from those of its fellow ceratopsians. They were broad instead of long, which may have helped it chew up all kinds of different vegetation. Each tooth had only one replacement tooth available — most ceratopsians had several teeth ready to take the place of one that was broken or fell out.

## Dinosaur Data

| | |
|---|---|
| PRONUNCIATION: | LEP-TOE-SERR-A-TOPS |
| SUBORDER: | MARGINOCEPHALIA |
| FAMILY: | PROTOCERATOPIDAE |
| DESCRIPTION: | SMALL AND AGILE HERBIVORE |
| FEATURES: | SMALL, FLAT NECK FRILL, PARROT-SHAPED BEAK |
| DIET: | LOW-LYING PLANTS |

# STYGIMOLOCH

## Fearsome-looking herbivore

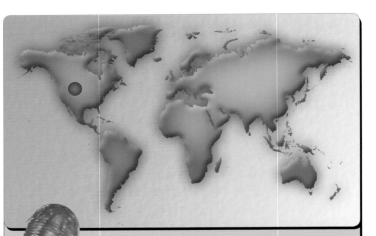

### FOSSIL FACTS
**Fossils have been found in Montana and Wyoming (USA). The first fossils were found in the 1800s, but the first complete skeleton was not found until 1995. It was discovered by fossil hunter Mike Triebold.**

### Appearance

Stygimoloch was a thick-skulled dinosaur with a dome-shaped head. It was a **biped**. Its arms were much shorter than its back legs, and it had five-fingered hands that would have helped it to

Stygimoloch means "demon from the River Styx" or "river devil." In Greek myth, the River Styx flowed through the underworld, called Hades (Hell).

The remains were found in a rock formation named "Hell Creek," so the dinosaur was named for the "hell river." Moloch was a fearsome Semitic god or demon – the ring of horns on Stygimoloch's head gave it, its finders thought, a demonic appearance.

grasp vegetation. Stygimoloch was a **herbivore**. It grazed the woodlands of North America 74–65 million years ago.

Its round head was covered in bony spikes and bumps, and it had a whole collection

of horns, some as long as 4 in. (10 cm). It was a small dinosaur, growing no more than 7–10 ft (2–3 m) long and most likely weighing no more than 220 lb (100 kg). It would have stood 4 ft (1.2 m) high.

The 1995 discovery of a complete Stygimoloch skeleton, and study of it, cast doubt on the long-held belief that Stygimoloch butted heads with one another like goats to battle for females or status within the herd.

The new find suggested that, if Stygimoloch had tried something like this, it would probably have broken its neck! Some scientists do still believe they may have headbutted other dinosaurs on their vulnerable underbellies, though. Others believe the spikes simply served to identify Stygimoloch to others of its kind.

# MEGA FACTS

- The first appearance of Stygimoloch in a film was in the Disney movie *Dinosaur* in 2000.

- It probably lived in herds.

- In 2003, Clayton Phipps found the world's only complete Stygimoloch skull. Its value is estimated at $150,000–$1million. Many scientists are opposed to the sale and auction of fossils, as it often results in specimens passing into private collections rather than public museums where they can be properly studied.

- The teeth in the back of its mouth resembled those of Stegosaurus, but the front of its mouth was full of sharp incisors, very like those of a carnivore.

## Dinosaur Data

| | |
|---|---|
| PRONUNCIATION: | STIG-IH-MOE-LOCK |
| SUBORDER: | CERAPODA |
| FAMILY: | PACHYCEPHALOSAURIA |
| DESCRIPTION: | SMALL, SPIKY HERBIVORE |
| FEATURES: | DOME-SHAPED HEAD, HORNS AND SPIKES |
| DIET: | LEAVES AND PLANTS |

# STYRACOSAURUS

## Spectacular horned herbivore

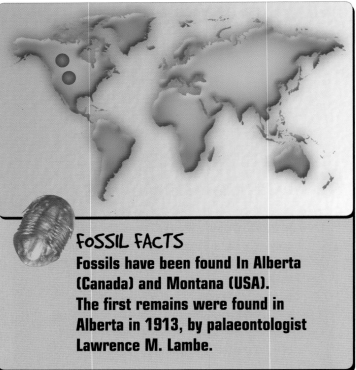

### FOSSIL FACTS
Fossils have been found In Alberta (Canada) and Montana (USA). The first remains were found in Alberta in 1913, by palaeontologist Lawrence M. Lambe.

short and strong, and Styracosaurus went on all fours. Unlike earlier frilled and horned dinosaurs, Styracosaurus' four-toed feet had blunt hoofs instead of claw-like ones. It had a massive head and a short, pointed tail.

It had a powerful, hooked beak, with teeth farther back in the side of its jaws, designed to let it tear and chew up the tough leaves of the low-growing plants on which it lived. Like other **ceratopsian** dinosaurs, it had large nasal openings in its deep snout – no one has yet discovered why this was useful to these creatures.

Styracosaurus means "spiked lizard". It had the most impressive set of horns ever seen in the animal kingdom – six long horns stuck out backwards from its neck frill, it had a smaller horn above each eye, and a single horn 2 ft (60 cm) long and 6 in. (15 cm) wide protruded from its nose!

### Appearance

Some 18 ft (5.5 m) in length and 6 ft (2 m) tall, Styracosaurus was about the size of an elephant and, like an elephant, its skin was tough and thick, making it a far from easy target for predators. It had a large, bulky body and could weigh up to 3 tons (3,000 kg). Its four sturdy legs were

Styracosaurus probably lived in herds, moving around their territory and feeding grounds slowly in large groups, and taking care of their young once they hatched. Large deposits of its fossilized bones (one contained some 100 Styracosaurus fossils!) have been found together in one area.

# MEGA FACTS

- Styracosaurus was an ancestor of Triceratops (see page 72).

- In spite of its bulk, scientists believe Styracosaurus might have been able to run at up to 20 mph (32 km/h) when it needed to! That's just a little faster than a car is allowed to go on the street where you live.

- A Styracosaurus was seen on film in 1969, badly miscast as a fearsome predator in *The Valley of Gwangi*. In 2000, it played a more peaceful role in the Walt Disney film *Dinosaur*.

- In May 2006, Styracosaurus took up residence in the toy section of the famous department store *Harrods*. Working full-time for seven weeks, two builders created a remarkable 825 lb (375 kg) LEGO model of the spiky dinosaur, using 180,000 LEGO bricks! It took them an incredible 506 hours to build, and the model is not only spectacular to see but can roar at passers-by from its setting of palm trees and tropical background noises.

## Dinosaur Data

| | |
|---|---|
| PRONUNCIATION: | STY-RACK-OH-**SAWR**-US |
| SUBORDER: | MARGINOCEPHALIA |
| FAMILY: | CERATOPSIDAE |
| DESCRIPTION: | HORNED AND FRILLED HERBIVORE |
| FEATURES: | SPECTACULAR HORNS, NECK FRILL, BEAK |
| DIET: | LOW-LYING PLANTS |

# EGGS AND LIFE CYCLE

## Eggs

Dinosaurs hatched from eggs laid by females. Dinosaur eggs were a variety of shapes and sizes, and could be up to 24 in. (60 cm) long. Even the biggest dinosaurs had small eggs, because the shell must be thin enough to allow oxygen in and the baby out. These eggs were similar to those of reptiles, birds and primitive mammals; they contained a **membrane** (called the amnion) that kept the embryo moist.

The first fossilized dinosaur eggs found (and the biggest to be found so far) were football-shaped eggs laid by Hypselosaurus (a member of the titanosaurus family, see page 110), found in France in 1869. These eggs were 12 in. (30 cm) long, had a volume of about 4 pints (2 liters) and may have weighed up to 15 lb (7 kg).

## Family life

Until recently the only real evidence of dinosaur family life were nests containing eggs from the Gobi Desert,

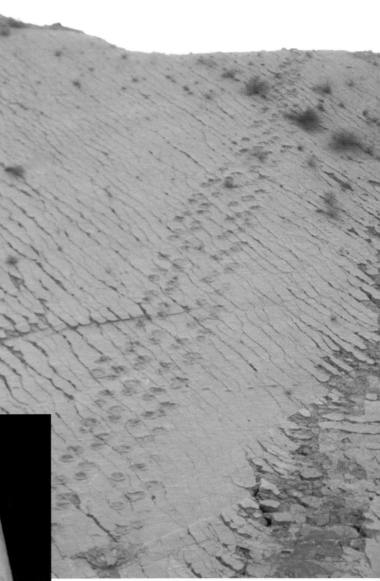

*Fossilized tracks*

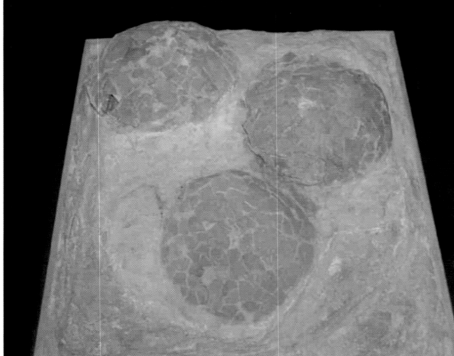

*Hypelosaurus egg fossils*

discovered in the 1920s and some tracks that showed adults and babies moving together. Very little is known about dinosaur courtship, rivalry, pairing and mating.

More than 200 dinosaur egg sites are now known around the world. The most recent discovery was about ten large dinosaur eggs (plus three egg impressions), found in 1999 in France. Larger egg sites have been found in Spain, where hundreds of thousands of eggs (of both **sauropods** and **theropods**) have been found. Dinosaur eggs sites have also been found in Argentina and China.

Very rarely, the eggs have preserved parts of embryos in them, which can help to match an egg with a species of dinosaur.

Nests, eggs, hatchlings, juveniles and adult Maiasauras (see page 100) were found in one area of the USA. This fossil evidence indicates a high level of parental care and a very social dinosaur.

Some dinosaurs cared for their eggs, others simply laid them and then abandoned them. It is thought that the nesting behavior of dinosaurs was very similar to the two types that modern birds display – "precocial" where babies leave the nest as soon as they hatch, and "altrical", where the helpless young remain in the nest. Dinosaurs also appeared to have some kind of homing instinct, like swallows or pigeons, that guided them back to the same breeding ground year after year.

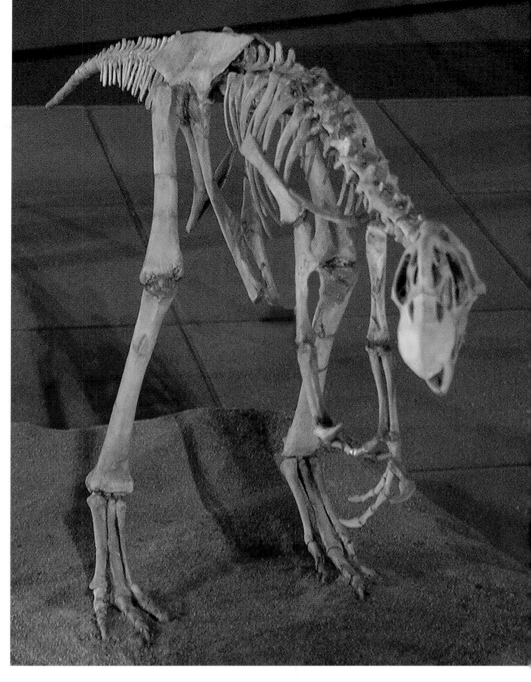

*Dinosaur skeleton*

## Reproduction

One of the many unanswered questions about dinosaur reproduction is how the giant sauropods like – Apatosaurus (see page 46), Diplodocus and Brachiosaurus (see page 40) laid their eggs without breaking them. Even if the sauropod squatted while laying eggs, the eggs would be dropped from a height of roughly 8 ft (2.5 m). Some scientists have argued that females may have had a tube that extended from the body for laying eggs (some modern day turtles have a tube like this).

*Maiasuara eggs*

# IGUANODON

## Thumb-spiked herbivore

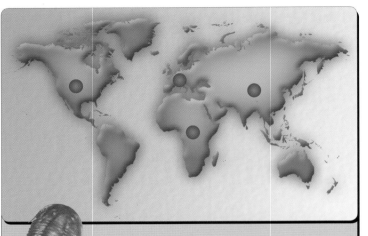

### FOSSIL FACTS
Fossils have been found in Europe, Africa, Asia, and North America. The first fossils were found in 1822, in Sussex (England).

### Dinosaur Data

| | |
|---|---|
| PRONUNCIATION: | IG-WAN-OH-DON |
| SUBORDER: | ORNITHOPODA |
| FAMILY: | IGUANODONTIDAE |
| DESCRIPTION: | SUCCESSFUL HERBIVORE |
| FEATURES: | HIGHLY-SPECIALISED HANDS, PARROT-LIKE BEAK |
| DIET: | CYCADS, CONIFER LEAVES, FERNS, HORSETAILS |

Iguanodon means "iguana tooth." It was named in 1825. Some of the first Iguanodon remains found were teeth, and they were very like those of the lizard Iguana – except the dinosaur teeth were 20 times bigger!

Iguanodon was the second dinosaur ever to be named. (Megalosaurus was first – see page 36).

## Appearance

Iguanodon had a bulky body, a stiff, flat tail, and a snout ending in a horny beak. It grew up to 33 ft (10 m) long, 16 ft (5 m) tall and stood 9 ft (2.78 m) high at the hip. It weighed up to 5 tons (5,000 kg).

There were no teeth in its horny beak but it did have cheek teeth further back, about 2 in. (5 cm) long.

It would use its beak to nip vegetation from trees and plants, then push its food farther back into its mouth to be ground up by the teeth. Iguanodon was unusual because it could actually chew its food. Most reptiles cannot do this. Iguanodon's specially-hinged upper jaw could flex from side to side, so its upper teeth ground over the lower ones.

Iguanodon had highly unusual forepaws. They could be used as hands for grasping, and also as feet for walking. The middle three fingers were linked together with webbing or padding (scientists are not sure which). The little finger was not linked to any other, and could curl and grasp things. Most unusual was the thumb – it was a sharp spike between 2 and 6 in. (5 and 15 cm) long. The purpose of this spike is still unclear – it may have been used for picking up and holding food, or (more likely) in self-defense.

Fossil footprints exist that show Iguanodon walking on all fours. But some scientists think it only grazed on four legs, and did most of its moving on just its hind legs. It had sturdy, pillar-like back legs, which were much longer than its slender front ones. The back feet had only three toes. Scientists agree that it could rear to get food, or run away. It may have been capable of running at speeds up to 9–12 mph (15–20 km/h)!

**Bonebed** discoveries where dozens of Iguanodon skeletons were found together show it was an animal that lived in herds.

# MEGA FACTS

- Iguanodon's razor-sharp thumb spike was at first thought to belong on its nose, as a kind of horn.

- Iguanodon bones have been found on nearly every continent of the world.

- An Iguanodon appears on the Coat of Arms of Maidstone, an English town close to where its fossils were found.

*An Iguanadon footprint*

# GALLIMIMUS

## Fast-moving bird-like dinosaur

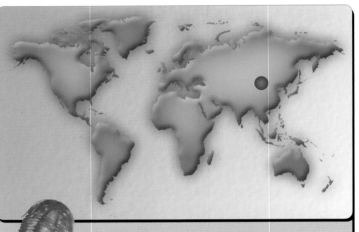

**FOSSIL FACTS**
**Fossils have been found in Asia.**
**The first fossils were discovered**
**in the early 1970s.**

Gallimimus means "chicken mimic" or "rooster mimic". It was named in 1972, for its resemblance to a huge bird.

### Appearance

It grew to a length of between 13 and 20 ft (4 and 6 m). It had a long neck, round head and prominent long, thin, and flat toothless beak. The bottom front part of its beak had a distinctive "shovel" shape. Its brain was comparatively large in relation to its body weight, making it one of the most intelligent of the dinosaurs. Its eyes were set on either side of its head, making depth perception impossible.

Gallimimus had hollow bones, but even so weighed some 880–1,100 lb (400–500 kg). It had a long tail that would help to stabilize it as it ran on its strong back legs.

### Diet

Gallimimus was closely related to **carnivorous** predators like Tyrannosaurus Rex (see page 24). It was thought until recently that it too probably preyed on small animals (like lizards) and used its beak to break open the eggs of other dinosaurs. In 2001, a fossil specimen was found showing that Gallimimus had peculiar tiny comb-like structures in its mouth. This plate strongly resembled the one a modern duck uses to "filter feed" – to filter out food particles from water.

This changed the way we think about Gallimimus' diet. Because fossils showed it to have weak jaw muscles, scientists supposed it ate stolen eggs or chased down weak prey. It is now believed Gallimimus may not have used its beak to kill prey at all.

# MEGA FACTS

- Gallimimus could probably run up to 43 mph (70 km/h)! That would make it the fastest dinosaur that ever lived.

- Unlike earlier "ostrich dinosaurs", Gallimimus had no teeth at all.

- We do not know for sure if it lived in herds or was a solitary creature.

It probably fed by straining food (tiny **invertebrates**, insects and plant material) out of water and sediment from the bottom of ponds and rivers. No one had expected to find evidence of filter-feeding in such large, land-based dinosaurs!

Gallimimus being a filter-feeder would make sense because its fossils have been found in rocks that would have been wet environments when it lived. It would also explain why the lower front part of its beak possesses a distinctive "shovel" shape.

## Dinosaur Data

| | |
|---|---|
| PRONUNCIATION: | GALL-IH-MIME-US |
| SUBORDER: | THEROPODA |
| FAMILY: | ORNITHOMIMIDAE |
| DESCRIPTION: | OSTRICH-LIKE **OMNIVORE** |
| FEATURES: | LONG LEGS, SMALL HEAD, FLEXIBLE NECK, PROMINENT BEAK |
| DIET: | MAY HAVE EATEN INSECTS, LIZARDS, EGGS, PLANTS OR STRAINED FOOD PARTICLES FROM WATER AND MUD |

# DRINKER

## Small bipedal herbivore

**BIRD·FOOTED DINOSAURS**

**FOSSIL FACTS**
**Drinker fossils have been found in the USA.**

## Dinosaur Data

| | |
|---|---|
| PRONUNCIATION: | DRINK-ER |
| SUBORDER: | ORNITHOPODA |
| FAMILY: | HYPSILOPHODONTIDAE |
| DESCRIPTION: | SMALL BIPEDAL HERBIVORE |
| FEATURES: | FLEXIBLE TAIL |
| DIET: | SWAMP VEGETATION AND PLANTS |

Drinker is named in honor of the scientist and dinosaur expert Edward Drinker Cope, who lived between 1840 and 1897.

Three partial skeletons of Drinker have been found. They are an adult, a youngster (or "subadult") and a child ("juvenile") so we can see what the dinosaur looked like at various stages of its life.

Drinker was quite a small dinosaur, growing to around 6 ft (2 m) long and 3 ft (1 m) high. It weighed only 55 lb (25 kg). Drinker was **bipedal**, had a flexible tail, and ate plants.

Drinker remains were found near those of marsh vegetation and lungfish teeth – so we think it lived near the swampy shores of lakes. Scurrying through swamps and forest undergrowth may have helped this little dinosaur hide from terrifying predators like Allosaurus (see page 34).

*Drinker*

# Edward Drinker Cope and the great bone wars

Cope poured his wealth into the search for dinosaur discoveries. His great rival was another famous **paleontologist** called Othniel Charles Marsh. The two men started out as friends, but in 1868 Cope discovered that Marsh had bribed the owners of a quarry which often sent dinosaur bones to Cope to send them to him

*Edward Drinker Cope (1840 – 97)*

(Marsh) instead. Thus was born a feud and rivalry between the two that would last almost 30 years and become known as "the Bone Wars".

The feud was worsened when Marsh pointed out that Cope had placed the head of his reassembled Elasmosaurus on the end of the skeleton's tail rather than its neck. Marsh made sure this mistake got plenty of publicity. The next year, Cope retaliated by luring away one of Marsh's assistants and having his people start digging in one of Marsh's excavations in Kansas.

The feud became a competition between the two, to see who could discover more new species of dinosaur and collect more fossil remains. The two scientists did very little excavation work themselves – they paid other collectors to do it for them. Cope once stole an entire train full of Marsh's

# MEGA FACTS

- Drinker might have lived in burrows close to marshes. Drinker had a flexible tail, unlike those of many dinosaurs, which would have allowed it to curl up in a burrow.

- Drinker had large feet, that helped it to move quickly and quietly.

fossils, and Marsh blew up one of his sites with dynamite rather than let Cope work there.

"The Bone Wars" lasted right up to the death of Cope in 1897. When Cope and Marsh began their work, only 18 dinosaur species were known in America – between them they raised this number to over 150.

*Othniel C. Marsh (1831 – 99)*

# LEAELLYNASAURA

## Sharp-eyed Antarctic herbivore

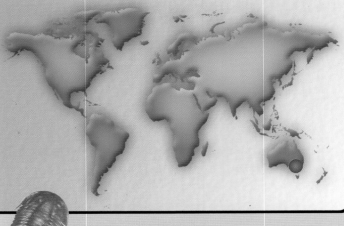

### FOSSIL FACTS
Fossils have been found in Australia. The first fossils were discovered in 1989.

### Dinosaur Data

| | |
|---|---|
| PRONUNCIATION: | LEE-ELL-LIN-AH-**SAWR**-AH |
| SUBORDER: | ORNITHOPODA |
| FAMILY: | HYPSILOPHODONTIDAE |
| DESCRIPTION: | SMALL BIPEDAL HERBIVORE |
| FEATURES: | HUGE EYES, BIG BRAIN, LONG HIND LEGS |
| DIET: | FERNS, MOSSES, HORSETAILS, LEAVES |

Leaellynasaura means "Leaellyn's lizard". It was named in 1989. Like Maiasaura (see page 100), it has the feminine Greek name-ending "-saura" rather than "-saurus."

This little **herbivore** was discovered first in Australia. In the late Cretaceous period, the continents were very different from the ones we recognize today. This part of Australia would have been well inside the Antarctic Circle, almost at the South Pole!

No reptile could live there today, but Leaellynasaura seemed to thrive there. Although the area was forested then, and days would have been fairly warm, the nights would have been long and cold. Leaellynasaura would have had to live without the sun for weeks or even months at a time!

Scientists believe Leaellynasaura lived in herds, and could have huddled together for warmth. That it could survive in the Antarctic cold and dark has even made some scientists think Leaellynsaura may have been warm-blooded.

## Appearance

An adult Leaellynasaura would have been about 8 ft (2.5 m) long, and only 18 in. (50 cm) tall at the hip. It weighed about 22 lb (10 kg). It stood on its hind legs (was **bipedal)** and had a long tail. Its hind legs were long and strong, as were its hind feet. Its front legs (its arms) were much shorter, and ended in hands.

Leallynasaura's 7 in. (17 cm) long skull shows that this dinosaur had very large eyes. The skull also has unusually large holes where the optic nerves connected back to the brain.

Scientists think Leaellynasaura must have had very good eyesight, and developed the ability to see in the dark thanks to living through dark Antarctic winters.

## Diet

Leaellynasaura had a tough horned beak. It probably fed on **horsetails**, mosses, and **ferns** which grew on the floor of the Antarctic forests. **Conifers** and **ginko** would have grown in the forests where it lived. It may even have scrambled up into trees to reach leaves. It would have used its beak to rip off leaves, then pushed them further back into its mouth, to be ground up by the cheek teeth in its strong jaws.

# MEGA FACTS

- We know from its skull that Leaellynasaura had a large brain compared to the size of its body — it was one smart dinosaur.

- Some scientists think Leaellynasaura survived the dark winter days by hibernating, like tortoises.

- Leaellynasaura built nests on the ground to lay their eggs in. A hatchling would have been only 12 in. (30 cm) long.

*Leaellynasaura*

# CAMPTOSAURUS

## Flexible reptile

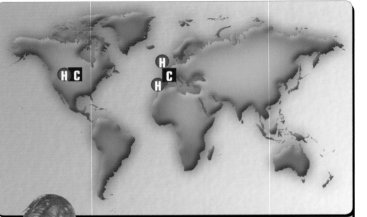

### FOSSIL FACTS

Camptosaurus fossils have been found in North America and Europe. Hypsilophodon fossils have been found in southern England, Spain, Portugal, and South Dakota (USA).

*Camptosaurus skeleton*

Othniel C. Marsh, the famous dinosaur hunter, named Camptosaurus in 1885, although it had first been discovered in 1879. Camptosaurus seem to have been quite widespread, as fossils have been found in Utah and Wyoming in the USA, and also in Oxfordshire, England, and in Portugal.

Camptosaurus was a heavy-bodied dinosaur, weighing up to 2 tons (2,000 kg), which could walk on all fours or rear up on its hind legs and balance to walk just on two feet. Standing, it could be up to 23 ft (7 m) tall. This was one of the first dinosaurs to have fleshy cheek pouches, like hamsters, for storing food in. It would have eaten **cycads**, ferns, and needles from pine trees.

### Dinosaur Data

| | |
|---|---|
| PRONUNCIATION: | KAMP-TOE-SORE-USS |
| SUBORDER: | ORNITHOPODA |
| DIET: | BIPEDAL PLANT EATER |

# HYPSILOPHODON

## High-ridged tooth

When it was first discovered in 1849 Hypsilophodon was thought to be a young Iguanodon (see page 86). However, in 1870 the **paleontologist** T.H. Huxley published a full description of Hypsilophodon and it was recognized as a different dinosaur.

Hypsilophodon was one of the smallest dinosaurs at around 6 ft (2 m) long and 154 lb (70 kg). It was **bipedal**, walking on two feet with only small forelimbs. Its heavy tail would have helped it to maintain its balance. It had 28 to 30 small, triangular, self-sharpening teeth to the front of its jaw for biting off leaves and ate low-growing plants and shrubs. Cheek pouches enabled it to store food for later, much like hamsters. Its small hands had five fingers each, with four toes on each foot. Having a lightweight body would have enabled it to move quite fast for its size, helping it to escape from Baronyx and Megalosaurus (see page 36), which probably hunted it for food.

*Hypsilophodon skeleton*

At one time it was thought that Hypsilophodon may have lived in trees but this theory was later disproved.

### Dinosaur Data

| | |
| --- | --- |
| PRONUNCIATION: | HIP-SILL-OWE-FOE-DON |
| SUBORDER: | ORNITHOPODA |
| DESCRIPTION: | LIGHTWEIGHT, FAST MOVER |
| DIET: | PLANT EATER |

# SKELETONS

Study of all dinosaurs starts with the skeletons. We have discovered several well-preserved skeletons to identify.

Anatomically, dinosaurs have skeletal features that distinguish them from other **archosaurs** such as crocodilians and **pterosaurs**. Dinosaurs have reduced fourth and fifth digits (like fingers) on their hands, their feet have three large toes, they have three or more vertebrae making up the sacrum (fused vertebrae by the hip), and have an open hip socket (a three-bone structure).

This hip structure gives dinosaurs a posture that positions their legs under their bodies, unlike other reptiles, which have legs that sprawl out to the sides. Dinosaurs were the first to be able to walk with straight legs tucked underneath their bodies. It has never been achieved by any other reptile before, or since, and it opened the way to the evolution of a variety of body types and lifestyles. This helped them to become the dominant land animals for 160 million years.

## Classification

Dinosaurs are classified by their hip structure, into the order saurischia (meaning lizard-hipped) and the order ornithischia (meaning bird-hipped). This division is based on their evolutionary tree; early in the Triassic period, dinosaurs branched into these two groups from their ancestors, the **thecodonts**.

## Skulls

The dinosaurs were diapsids (as are all reptiles except turtles), which are animals that had two extra holes in the sides of their skulls.

Dinosaur skeletons differed from species to species. Utahraptor, (a member of the **therapod** family), was a swift and terrifying predator that stood taller than a man. Its skeleton was lightly built, making it swift and able to move about easily, while its long tail helped it to balance. This allowed it to perform acrobatic feats, such as jumping and balancing on one foot.

*Hypsilophodon*

## Hypsilophodon

Hypsilophodon was a two-legged plant eater standing just 5 ft (1.5 m) high. The most striking feature about a Hypsilophodon skeleton is how little there is of it. Rather like a gazelle or antelope, the whole structure had been slimmed down to give maximum support for minimum weight. Even the bones were thin-walled and hollow, just like a gazelle's. A Hypsilophodon's thighbone was quite short, allowing it to be pulled rapidly back and forth for fast strides.

## Tyrannosaurus Rex

Giant meat eater Tyrannosaurus Rex had a bulky body, a big head with powerful jaws, sharp teeth, and a stiff tail. Its front legs were tiny. It probably had about 200 bones, roughly the same as a human (no one knows exactly how many it had, since no complete Tyrannosaurus skeletons have been found). Scientists cannot agree whether Tyrannosaurus was capable of fast movement or not. Its skeleton is heavy and does not suggest a fast mover, but the upper foot bones are locked together for strength, possibly to withstand the stresses of running, indicating that perhaps it was a fast-moving animal.

*Dinosaur skull showing two extra holes in sides of skull*

*Complete mounted dinosaur skeleton from the Natural History Museum, London*

# CORYTHOSAURUS

## Crested duck-billed herbivore

**FOSSIL FACTS**
**Fossils have been found in western North America and Canada. The first fossils were discovered in Alberta in 1912 by Barnum Brown.**

The purpose of Corythosaurus' helmet-shaped crests has been much debated by scientists. Some think that it served display purposes (adult males had larger head crests than juveniles or females) and recognizing other Corythosaurus. Fossil remains of Corythosaursus have been found mixed together with those of other herbivores, suggesting that sometimes herds of different kinds of herbivore may have mingled together while migrating or grazing. If so, it would have been very useful to be able to recognize other members

Corythosaurus means "helmet lizard." This duck-billed dinosaur was named by Barnum Brown in 1914, for the hollow bony crest on top of its large head, shaped and flattened at the sides like a helmet.

## Appearance

Corythosaurus grew to some 33 ft (10 m) long, standing 6 ft (2 m) high at the hip. It weighed around 4 tons (4,000 kg). Its arms were very much shorter than its back legs, and it is thought it could rise up on its hind legs and feet to look around for danger, and to run at a moderately fast pace. Its long pointed tail would help it balance. Fossilized footprints suggest that most of the time it went on all fours, foraging for low-growing plants. It would crop such plants with the toothless beak at the end of its long, narrow snout. Food would then be pushed back farther, to be ground up by hundreds of sharp cheek teeth. These teeth were constantly replaced as they wore down and fell out.

of the Corythosaurus herd by looking for the distinctive crest on the head. Its enhanced sense of smell would also have helped it recognize and find its own kind.

Almost all scientists now agree that Corythosaurus also used the air chamber inside the crest to communicate by emitting sounds rather like a trumpet. The call of the Corythosaurus would have been booming and deep and carried great distances through the prehistoric forests.

# MEGA FACTS

- In 1916, the Canadian ship *Mount Temple* was carrying two specimens of Corythosaurus from Canada to Britain when it was sunk by the German submarine *SMS Moewe*. Its prehistoric cargo now lies at the bottom of the North Atlantic.

- It is the duck-billed dinosaur about which we know most, since over 20 skulls have been found.

- Scientists once thought this dinosaur lived mostly in the water, as it appeared to have webbed feet and hands. Later study showed that the 'webs' were simply deflated padding.

- Corythosaurus lived between the western mountains of North America and an inland sea. It may have migrated from the shoreline to higher ground to reproduce.

## Dinosaur Data

| | |
|---|---|
| PRONUNCIATION: | COR-IH-THOH-SAWR-US |
| SUBORDER: | ORNITHOPODA |
| FAMILY: | HADROSAURIDAE |
| DESCRIPTION: | CRESTED HERBIVORE |
| FEATURES: | HELMET-SHAPED CREST |
| DIET: | PINE NEEDLES, CONIFERS, GINKGOS, TWIGS, LEAVES, FRUITS |

# MAIASAURA

## Migratory duck-billed dinosaur

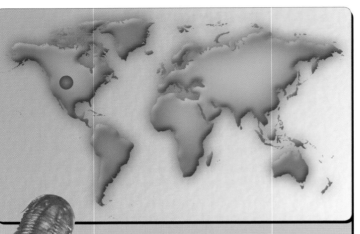

**FOSSIL FACTS**
**Fossils have been found in Montana (USA). The first fossils were found in 1977, on a ranch near Choteau, Montana.**

It grew to around 30 ft (9.2 m) long and weighed 3–4 tons (3,000–4,000 kg) when fully grown. It went on all four legs most of the time, but may have been able to raise up onto its hind legs to reach vegetation or to run away from predators. Its arms were much shorter than the strong back legs.

## Family life

Large numbers of fossils from this dinosaur have been found together (one site contained 10,000!) including eggs, nests, and babies. Scientists therefore believe Maiasaura was a herding animal. The discovery of this dinosaur revolutionized the way we think about how dinosaurs raised their young, challenging the traditional view of them as uncaring reptiles that largely left their eggs and young to fend for themselves.

The most famous find was made on a site that has become known as "Egg Mountain". This site had preserved a group of Maiasaura nests, and one of these contained bones from babies some weeks old. That these babies were still in

Maiasaura means "good mother lizard". It was named by **paleontologist** Jack Horner, after he discovered a series of nests with the remains of both eggs and hatchlings in them. This was the first proof that some giant dinosaurs raised and fed their young.

## Appearance

Maiasaura was a **hadrosaur** that inhabited the coastal lowlands of Montana some 75 million years ago. Unlike some hadrosaurs, it had only a tiny crest on its head – it also had small bony spikes above each eye. Its face was long and broad, ending in a short, wide bill. Its flat skull measured up to 33 in. (82 cm) long and 14 in. (35 cm) high. Its beak was toothless, but Maiasaura had many self-sharpening teeth farther back in its cheeks to grind up vegetation.

*Maiasaura skeleton*

MAIASAURA PEEBLESORUM
Baby and sub-adult skeletons (76,500,000)
Hatchling and 4 year old Maiasaura, illustrating the incredible
rate of growth these kinds of dinosaurs achieved. Maiasaura
took 7 to 8 years to reach average adult size.
TETON COUNTY, MONTANA (TNC)

the nest so long after hatching showed that the parent dinosaurs must have been looking after them. Babies were about 14 in. (35 cm) long when they hatched and grew to 10 ft (3 m) by the end of their first year, an impressively fast rate of growth.

Large amounts of plant remains have been found around fossilized eggs, and in fact vegetation may have been placed over the eggs to help incubate them — the rotting vegetation would generate heat.

# MEGA FACTS

- In 1985, a bone fragment from Maiasaura was flown into space during an eight-day NASA experiment for Skylab 2.

- Maiasaura is the official state fossil of Montana.

## Dinosaur Data

| | |
|---|---|
| PRONUNCIATION: | MY-AH-SAWR-AH |
| SUBORDER: | ORNITHOPODA |
| FAMILY: | HADROSAURIDAE |
| DESCRIPTION: | MEDIUM-SIZED DUCK-BILLED DINOSAUR |
| FEATURES: | TINY SKULL CREST, LARGE SKULL, BROAD BILL |
| DIET: | LOW-GROWING VEGETATION AND SOME HIGHER LEAVES |

# EDMONTOSAURUS

## Toothy duck-billed tree browser

**DUCKBILLS**

Edmontosaurus means "lizard from Edmonton". It was named in 1917.

### Appearance

Edmontosarous was 43 ft (13 m) long and weighed around 3.5 tons (3,500 kg). It had the flat and sloping head common to many duck-billed dinosaurs, and its mouth was a wide spoon-like beak.

The beak was toothless, but packed tightly back in the cheeks were six rows containing hundreds of teeth – Edmontosaurus would have been able to grind up very tough food by moving it across these teeth and back from muscular cheek pouches. As soon as a tooth wore out, it was replaced.

This tree-browsing **herbivore** would have gone on all four legs to graze, but was probably able to stand up on its powerful hind legs and move on just those two legs. Its front legs were shorter and less powerful.

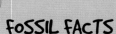

### FOSSIL FACTS
Fossils have been found in the USA and Canada. The first fossils were discovered in 1912.

## Dinosaur Data

| | |
|---|---|
| PRONUNCIATION: | ED-MON-TOE-SAWR-US |
| SUBORDER: | ORNITHOPODA |
| FAMILY: | HADROSAURIDAE |
| DESCRIPTION: | TREE-BROWSING DUCK-BILLED DINOSAUR |
| FEATURES: | HUNDREDS OF TEETH, LOOSE SKIN BALLOON |
| DIET: | CONIFER NEEDLES, SEEDS, TWIGS |

*Edmontosaurus*

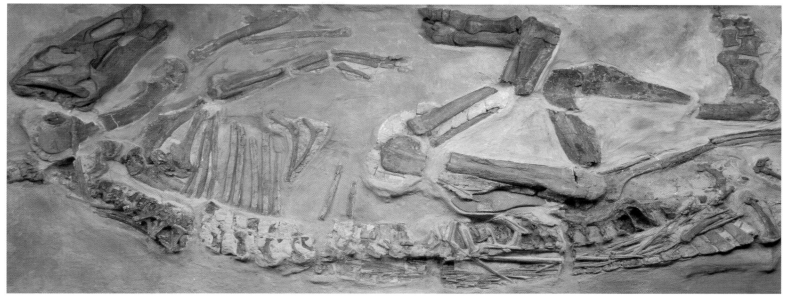

*Edmontosaurus skeleton*

## Defense

Edmontosaurus was slow-moving, and possessed few defenses – it may have had good eyesight, hearing and smell to help it keep out of the way of predators who shared the same time and territory, such as Tyrannosaurus Rex (see page 24). We also know, from some remarkable mummified fossil remains found in 1908, that Edmontosaurus had tough, scaly skin, with a row of bumps (called tubercles) running along its neck, back and tail.

With few ways to defend themselves, these herbivores were likely to have sought safety by banding together in herds. In Alberta (Canada) a mass "graveyard" of Edmontosaurus fossils supports the idea that they lived in herds. They may have migrated with the seasons, from the North Slope of Alaska (where plants to eat would have been scarce in the dark months of winter) to the richer, swampy area of Alberta.

## MEGA FACTS

- An Edmontosaurus fossil now displayed in the Denver Museum of Nature and Science shows evidence of a Tryannosaurus Rex bite to the tail. Astonishingly, the bone shows signs of healing – the Edmontosaurus apparently lived through the attack. This evidence of healing proved that Tyrannosaurus Rex's prey was alive when bitten, which means Tryannosaurus Rex was not a pure scavenger as was suggested in the 1970s.

- As Edmontosaurus herds migrated, Tryannosaurus Rex probably followed its food source, snatching weaker or older members of the herd as "ready meals."

- When first found, many scientists thought Edmontosaurus must have spent a lot of its time in the water, as its hands seemed to be webbed. None of the other evidence we have argues for an aquatic lifestyle, however, and it seems that the "webs" were simply collapsed padding that had once cushioned the feet and hands.

# PARASAUROLOPHUS

## Toothy duck-billed tree-browser

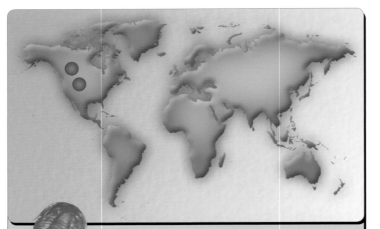

**FOSSIL FACTS**
**Fossils have been found in Canada and the USA. The first fossil was found in Alberta in 1922.**

Parasaurolophus means "near crested lizard". It was named by Dr. William A. Parks, in 1922. It lived in the jungles of North America 75–65 million years ago.

### Appearance

Parasaurolophus had the most remarkable skull crest of any of its kind. The crest extending from the back of its skull could be up to 6 ft (1.8 m) long and was a hollow tube filled with passages that connected its nostrils right back to the tip of the crest.

Parasaurolophus was one of the largest **herbivores** of the Cretaceous period. It grew up to 33 ft (10 m) long and 16 ft (4.9 m) high, and weighed around 3.5 tons (3,500 kg). Its front legs were shorter than its back legs – it probably went on all fours when foraging for low-growing plants, but could rise up onto its back legs, using its long tail to help balance, to look around, reach higher leaves, or run away from predators. It had no real

### Dinosaur Data

| | |
|---|---|
| PRONUNCIATION: | PAR-AH-**SAWR**-OH-**LOW**-FUSS |
| SUBORDER: | ORNITHOPODA |
| FAMILY: | HADROSAURIDAE |
| DESCRIPTION: | BIZARRELY-CRESTED DUCKBILLED HERBIVORE |
| FEATURES: | MASSIVE SKULL CREST |
| DIET: | LEAVES, TWIGS, PINE NEEDLES |

means to defend itself besides running away, and probably sought safety in numbers by living in herds.

Its long neck would allow it to reach food either on the ground or up in the trees.

It had a duck-like beak at the front of its snout that would allow it to slice off leaves and other vegetation – all its teeth were further back, in its cheeks, where food would be pushed to be ground up into mush. Its snout was narrow, and shorter than those of most other duck-billed dinosaurs.

## Parasaurolophus' "voice"

Parasaurolophus' amazing crest contained a maze of air chambers that connected back to the breathing passages.

Most scientists believe this allowed the crest to be used as a "resonating chamber", which let the dinosaur make loud, low-frequency sounds by blowing air through it. In 1995 a study in New Mexico was begun using powerful computers and CT scans of a fossil skull to

actually recreate the sound that Parasaurolophus would have made. In 1997, the recreated "song of the dinosaur" was heard again for the first time in 75 million years. Parasaurolophus emitted a low-frequency rumbling sound, which could change in pitch. It's even thought that this "voice" was distinctive enough to distinguish individual Parasaurolophus from one another, not just from other types of dinosaur!

# MEGA FACTS

- Its brain was about the size of a human fist.

- Fossils of the large bones in its ears suggest it would have been able to hear sounds below the range of human hearing.

- Fossil remains have shown us that Parasaurolophus' hide was tough and pebbly.

Parasaurolophus skeleton

# GRYPOSAURUS

## Griffin lizard

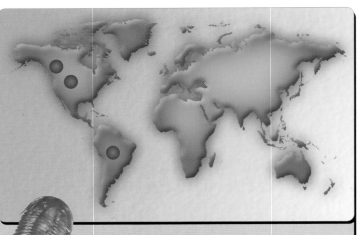

**FOSSIL FACTS**
Fossils have been found in Canada and the USA and possibly South America.

At around 30 ft (9 m) tall and weighing up to 3 tons (3,000 kg), Gryposaurus is regarded as a medium-sized hadrosaur. Fossilized skulls and bones show that Gryposaurus would have had a very distinctively shaped nose with very curved upward-facing nostrils and a very prominent and angular nose. The head itself was long and narrow with a characteristic duckbill jaw.

## Skin

Fossilized impressions of its skin were discovered together with bones. Gryosaurus skin was made up of small scales,

## Dinosaur Data

| | |
|---|---|
| PRONUNCIATION: | GRIP-OWE-SORE-USS |
| SUBORDER: | ORNITHOPODA |
| FAMILY: | HADROSAUR |
| DESCRIPTION: | DUCK-BILLED PLANT-EATER |

each less than a third of an inch (1 cm) across. These small scales would have covered and protected its whole body, although they would probably have been a little larger on its tail.

*Gryposaurus*

# MEGA FACTS

- Standing tall on its hind legs, Gryposaurus would have been able to take leaves, pine needles, and twigs from quite high up in the trees. Cheek teeth would have helped it to chew its food well.

- Many dinosaurs have been found in the same rock formation as Gryposaurus, the Two Medicine Formation in Montana.

# DIMORPHODON

## Primitive fish-eating winged reptile

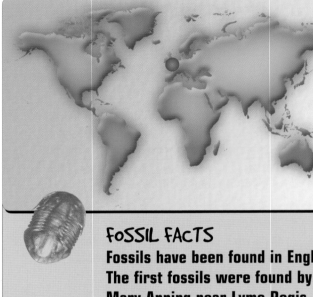

### FOSSIL FACTS
**Fossils have been found in England. The first fossils were found by Mary Anning near Lyme Regis in 1828.**

The name Dimorphodon means "two-form teeth". It was named by **paleontologist** Sir Richard Owen in 1859. It has two distinct kinds of teeth – those at the front are longer than those at the back.

### Appearance

Dimorphodon was actually a winged reptile called a **pterosaur** that lived at the same time as the dinosaurs.

It is one of the earliest pterosaurs that have been discovered, living 206–180 million years ago, and quite a small one at 3 ft (1 m) long. Its wings were formed by a leathery membrane which stretched between its body, the top of its legs, and its fourth finger. Its hollow bones made it light in the air.

It had a massive head, with wide and deep jaws. The head was extremely large compared to the rest of the body, and it is thought the large beak may have been colored, making it useful for display to other Dimorphodons. Like all pterosaurs, it had huge eyes and so probably excellent eyesight.

At the other end of its body was a long, pointed tail, which ended in a curious diamond-shaped flap of skin. This tail may have helped stabilize the creature while in the air, or helped to balance it while walking on the ground.

### Dinosaur Data

| | |
|---|---|
| PRONUNCIATION: | DIE-MORF-OH-DON |
| SUBORDER: | RHAMPHORYNCHOIDEA |
| FAMILY: | DIMORPHODONTIDAE |
| DESCRIPTION: | PRIMITIVE WINGED REPTILE |
| FEATURES: | TWO DIFFERENT KINDS OF TEETH IN ITS BEAK |
| DIET: | FISH, INSECTS, AND POSSIBLY SMALL ANIMALS |

# MEGA FACTS

- It had a wingspan of 6 ft (1.7m).

- The specimen found by Mary Anning is believed to have been the first complete pterosaur skeleton ever discovered.

- It may have used its increased leg span to hold onto cliffs while waiting for fish to surface – then swooped down to catch its next meal.

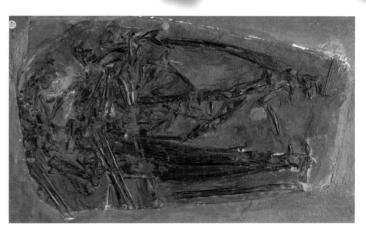

*Dimorphodon skull*

## How it moved

There is disagreement about how Dimorphodon moved when it was not flying. Fossil tracks seem to suggest that it went on all fours, but some scientists think it was capable of standing fully or semi-upright on its hind legs and even running quite fast. Unlike most other pterosaurs, Dimorphodon had legs which rather stuck out to the sides, which would have given it a somewhat clumsy, waddling gait. This leads some **paleontologists** to suggest it may have spent most of its time off the ground, hanging from tree branches or cliffs, using its grasping hands and toe claws to hold on.

It has often been thought that Dimorphodon would have been able to run very fast, rising up onto its toes to do so. Recently discovered fossil evidence, though, suggests that it was actually incapable of bending its foot – it would have been flat-footed and needed to place either all or none of its foot on the ground.

*Dimorphodon fossilized skeleton*

# CAUDIPTERYX

## Flightless feathered dinosaur

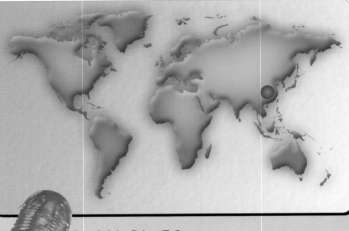

### FOSSIL FACTS
**Fossils were found in the Liaoning Province of China in 1997 and identified by Philip Currie.**

Caudipteryx means "tail feather" or "winged tail"and refers to this dinosaur's short, feathered tail plume.

### Appearance

Caudipteryx was a small **bipedal** dinosaur, with long legs, a pair of very short arms, and a short tail. It was about 3 ft (1m) tall and weighed about the same as a large turkey. Its short snout contained long sharp teeth. Its long legs and relatively light weight would have made it a very fast runner.

Its body was covered in short, downy feathers and had longer, quill-like feathers on its arms and tail. The tail feathers were up to 8 in. (20 cm) long and arranged in a fan or plume. It is thought that Caudipteryx could have used this tail plume for display. Although Caudipteryx's arms had long, quill-like feathers and looked much more like small wings than arms, it could not fly.

Caudipteryx's feathers were still very useful to it as they would have provided good insulation. They may have also been useful for aggressive displays or to attract a mate, as well as allowing it to warm its eggs.

### Diet

Caudipteryx lived in wetlands, so it probably waded in the water to catch small fish in its sharp-toothed mouth. However, fossils have been found with tiny stones in their stomach. These gastroliths are used to help digest vegetable matter, suggesting its diet consisted at least partially of plants. It is possible that it had a diet consisting of plants, small fish, and other small animals.

## Dinosaur Data

| | |
|---|---|
| PRONUNCIATION: | CAW-DIP-TER-IKS |
| SUBORDER: | THEROPODA |
| FAMILY: | CAUDIPTERIDAE |
| DESCRIPTION: | LONG-LEGGED FEATHERED DINOSAUR |
| FEATURES: | DISTINCTIVE TAIL PLUME, FEATHERS AND WING-LIKE ARMS |
| DIET: | SMALL FISH |

# MEGA FACTS

- Caudipteryx's teeth faced outward, giving it a distinctly buck-toothed appearance.

- Caudipteryx is one of many excellent fossil samples to have been discovered in the Liaoning province of China. These finds are especially exciting because of their excellent state of preservation – some even have impressions of skin and feathers, even indicating patterns like banding that help us to understand what dinosaurs really looked like.

## Evolution of Birds

Most scientists now accept that birds evolved from dinosaurs. However, some believe that all birds descended from a creature called Archaeopteryx (see page 112). Others believe that modern birds evolved from the maniraptors, a group whose early members included Caudipteryx and whose later members included Velociraptor (see page 32) and Deinonychus (see page 28). These later members had evolved the swiveling wrist bone joint that is necessary for flight.

Caudipteryx's feathers and wing-like arms suggest that it might be the missing link in the evolution of birds from dinosaurs!

# ARCHAEOPTERYX

## Winged and feathered bipedal carnivore

### FOSSIL FACTS
**Fossils have been found in Bavaria, Germany.**

| Bird-like features | Dinosaur-like features |
|---|---|
| Feathered wings with reduced finger | Claws on wings, could be used to grasp |
| Wishbone | Teeth |
| Bird-like brain | Long bony tail |
| Hollow bones | Jaws (not a beak!) |
| Feathers on body and tail | |

*This table gives details of the features that Archaeopteryx shared with birds and dinosaurs.*

In 2004, an experiment was carried out at the National History Museum in London to try to answer this question. Scanning equipment was used to scan the brain case of an Archaeopteryx skull. The brain shape was much more like that of a modern bird than the brain of a dinosaur.

Archaeopteryx means "ancient feather." It was named by Hermann von Meyer in 1861. Archaeopteryx is often said to be a link between dinosaurs and birds.

### Appearance

Archaeopteryx was magpie-sized, weighing around 12 oz (325 g). It had short, broad wings and a long tail and neck. Its jaws were lined with sharp cone-shaped teeth. It had long legs, with long thighs and short calves. Its wings, body, and tail were feathered. Its large eyes would have given it excellent vision. It had feathers and wings like a bird, but teeth, skeleton, and claws like a dinosaur.

In 2005, a particularly well-preserved fossil specimen was studied. The second toe could be stretched much more than the rest, rather like the special "retractable" claws of Velociraptor (see page 32). The hind toe was not "reversed" like a thumb on a grasping hand, and so Archaeopteryx could not have used it to cling onto branches.

### Could Archaeopteryx fly?

Scientists have argued over whether or not this animal could fly ever since the first Archaeopteryx fossil was found. If it could fly, did it just flap its wings weakly, or fly strongly?

*Archaeopteryx fossil*

# MEGA FACTS

- Only ten Archaeopteryx fossils exist, and only one feather sample.

- Archaeopteryx's brain was only the size of a conker. But the size of its brain compared to its body was three times as big as that of similar sized reptiles.

- It had a wingspan of 18 in. (50 cm).

- There were flying dinosaurs before and after Archaeopteryx, but they had skin, not feathers, on their wings.

The areas controling vision and movements were enlarged, just like a bird's, and the inner ear (which controls balance) was also like a bird's. It was a brain designed for flight and balance!

Dr. Angela Milner, who carried out the study, believes this is strong evidence that Archaeopteryx could and did fly. Most scientists now agree that archaeopteryx *could* fly, but was a weak flyer.

## Dinosaur Data

| | |
| --- | --- |
| PRONUNCIATION: | ARK-EE-OP-TER-IKS |
| SUBORDER: | THERAPODA |
| FAMILY: | ARCHAEOPTERIDAE |
| DESCRIPTION: | FEATHERED BIPEDAL CARNIVORE |
| FEATURES: | FEATHERED WINGS |
| DIET: | INSECTS, SMALL CREATURES |

# PTERANODON INGENS

## Winged and toothless flying reptile

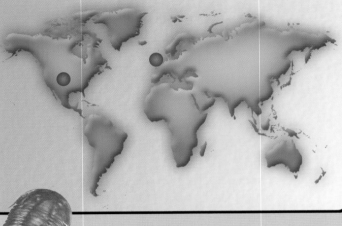

### Dinosaur Data

| | |
|---|---|
| PRONUNCIATION: | TER-AN-O-DON |
| SUBORDER: | PTERODACTYLOIDEA |
| FAMILY: | PTERADONTIDAE |
| DESCRIPTION: | CARNIVORE |
| FEATURES: | HUGE WINGSPAN |
| DIET: | FISH, MOLLUSCS, CRABS, INSECTS |

It probably looked more like a huge bat than a bird, with large, soft hair-covered membranes for wings. The membrane itself was very thin but extremely strong and stretched out between the body and the tops of its legs. These flying reptiles did not have any feathers.

Pteranodon lived at the same time as Tyrannosaurus Rex. It was not a true dinosaur but was related to them.

Pteranodon had a wing span of up to 30–33 ft (9–10 m) and weighed around 44–55 lb (20–25 kg).

FLYING DINOSAURS

It would have been able to walk on the ground but, once in the air, Pteranodon would have looked like a huge glider. Pteranodon could fly long distances using its large light-weight wings; it would have taken advantage of rising thermals to soar over the swampy forest below.

# MEGA FACTS

- It used the large bony crest on its head to steer when flying.

- Their brightly-colored crests were larger in the male and were used for attracting females and indicating readiness to mate.

- Their lower jaw was over 3 ft (1 m) in length.

- They would have been agile, elegant, and quite fast when flying, reaching speeds up to 30 mph (48 km/h).

## Diet

It had no teeth but was **carnivorous**. Fossil skeletons found near the edge of the sea show that fish was probably an important part of its diet. Its scoop-like beak would have helped it swoop down to catch fish straight from near the surface of the water. Its excellent eyesight would have helped it to see fish in the water as it flew above the surface.

# HESPERORNIS

## Flightless toothed marine dinosaur

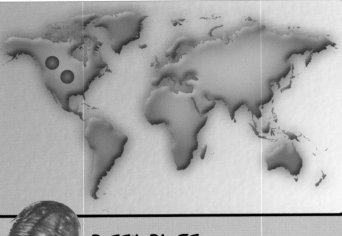

**FOSSIL FACTS**
Fossils have been found in the USA and Canada. The first fossils were found in 1871.

Hesperornis means "western bird." It was named in 1871 by the **paleontologist** Othniel C. Marsh. The discovery of Hesperornis was very important, because it filled a big gap in the fossil history of birds.

Hesperornis is part of a group of dinosaurs called the hesperornithiforms. These were the only true marine dinosaurs of the whole Mesozoic era. Dinosaurs that lived in the sea seem to have lived only in the northern hemisphere and were flightless diving birds. They would have dived to catch fish.

## Appearance

Hesperornis looked a lot like a bird with teeth. It grew to about 5 ft (1.5 m) long and it had small and useless wings (which scientists call *vestigal* wings). It had sprawling back legs, set very far back on the body. These long legs ended in webbed feet. It had a big head on the end of a long neck. Its long beak was set with simple, sharp teeth along its bottom jaw, and at the back of its upper jaw.

A different kind of hesperornithiform, called Parahesperornis, has been found showing the imprinted remains of thick, hairy feathers. It is likely that Hesperornis, too, had such feathers. They would not have helped it fly, but would have done a good job of keeping it warm.

In the water, Hesperornis was a powerful swimmer and diver. Unlike modern flightless birds like penguins, it did not use its wings as well as its feet to push itself through the water. Its wings were tiny and of no use, but its back

### Dinosaur Data

| | |
|---|---|
| PRONUNCIATION: | HES-PER-OR-NIS |
| SUBORDER: | ODONTORNITHES |
| FAMILY: | HESPERORNITHIDAE |
| DESCRIPTION: | FLIGHTLESS TOOTHED DIVING BIRD |
| FEATURES: | VESTIGAL WINGS, TOOTHED BEAK |
| DIET: | FISH, SQUID, AMMONITES |

legs were powerful. The wings may have been useful for steering when diving underwater. It had dense (heavy) bones that made it less buoyant and helped it to dive. Its sleek, feathered body was well designed for moving smoothly through the water.

On land, Hesperornis was awkward and clumsy. Thanks to the position of its hip bones and back legs, it may not even have been able to stand up and waddle about on dry land. It would have moved on land by sliding about on its belly, pushing with those strong back legs. It probably only went up on land to nest and lay eggs. For safety, it probably nested in groups and chose inaccessible, rocky spots.

# MEGA FACTS

- Hesperornis remains have been found in the fossilized stomachs of mosasaur (see page 16) skeletons.

- Hesperornis was the largest of the flightless diving birds of the late Cretaceous period.

- Unable to fly or walk, Hesperornis was in danger from predators both in the water and on land.

# FORMATION OF FOSSILS

A fossil means the traces of any past life preserved in the rocks. Fossilization takes millions of years. When a dinosaur died, normally the bones started to fall apart. If, however, the body was quickly covered with a layer of earth, this process did not occur.

Once the sediment had covered the dinosaur, its soft parts disappeared over time and only the hard bones and teeth were left behind.

The sediment gradually built up on top of the bones, forming part of rocks such as limestone, mudstone, sandstone, clay, or shale. Minerals from water around the rocks seeped into the bone structure, which gradually changed into rock.

Millions of years later the fossil appeared as the covering rock was worn away by wind and water.

There are only a few fossils of dinosaurs because they were land animals, and it is normally sea creatures that were fossilized as the silt at the bottom of the sea or a lake covered the remains.

## How fossils are made

There are a number of ways in which dinosaur remains can become fossils. When sediment covers bones and minerals seep into the bones, it gradually turns into rock. These fossils, part original bone and part rock, are called "petrified".

*Ankylosaurus*

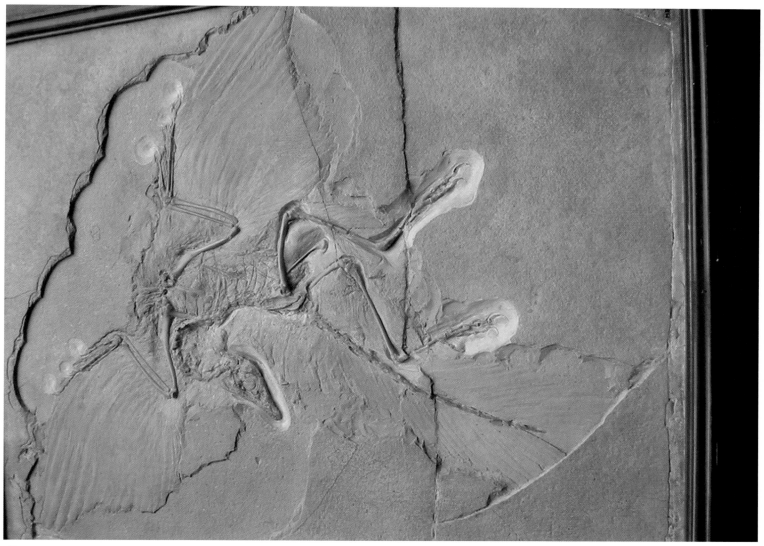

*Ramphoryncus fossils*

Sometimes acidic water dissolved the bone and left a hollow space (mold) where the bone used to be. These are "natural mold" fossils and, by pouring material such as plaster of Paris or rubber latex into them, the exact shape of the bone can be recreated.

In other cases, these natural molds are filled later with sediments or different minerals such as silica, calcite, or iron pyrites which gradually built up a perfect copy (replica). These are "natural cast" fossils.

Sometimes a dead animal is buried between layers of rock, which form an impression or cast that can be split apart along the layer containing the bones, producing a part and counterpart. In a few cases, the casts include impressions of feathers or skin that decayed long ago.

The rarest fossil of all formed when the dinosaur's body had been covered in a dry environment and some of the soft parts had become preserved (mummified) and then fossilized. In these cases, the skin texture, and even the folds in it, can be clearly seen. The color is not preserved, though, as it takes on the color of the surrounding rocks.

*Construction of a replica skeleton of Titanosaurus*

## Other fossils

Apart from dinosaur remains, other fossils of the dinosaurs exist, such as fossilized footprints or tracks, nests and eggs, scratches in the ground, toothmarks on bones, dung, stomach stones, and much more. These can tell us about how the dinosaurs lived and behaved, not just what they looked like. For example, footprints and tracks tell us whether dinosaurs lived alone or in groups, and how fast they moved.

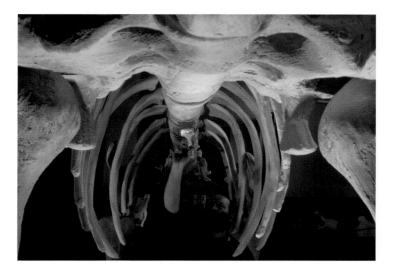

# FOSSIL HUNTING

The only knowledge of dinosaurs comes from fossils. These are often parts of skeletons, but footprints, eggs and, occasionally, remains of skin and even droppings have been found.

The discovery of a site can happen by accident – for example, discovering remains while carrying out other work – or alternatively by planned digging with the aim of finding fossils.

Dinosaurs inhabited all the continents, although at that time the continents were in different places from where they are now. The climates were also quite different. Most fossils are those of sea animals, particularly those that lived in shallow water near the coast, where mud and silt were constantly present to bury their dead remains. As dinosaurs were all land animals, there are very few fossils because their bodies were usually eaten by scavengers or scattered in the wind. If the remains were covered quickly, however, a few fossils survived. Sometimes the remains were washed into a nearby stream or river and eventually found their way into a lake or seabed, where they became fossilized.

## First fossils

The first dinosaur fossils to be studied scientifically came from western England. The countries where particularly large numbers of dinosaur remains have been found include the United States, Canada, China, Mongolia, Argentina, and Tanzania. However, not all of the regions of the world have been investigated fully.

## Extraction of fossils

**Paleontologists** uncovering a site containing the remains of dinosaurs use techniques that enable them to extract the fossils in the best possible condition. These techniques ensure that we can gather the best possible information about the fossils and prevent any damage during transport to the laboratory to analyze them. There, the fossils are prepared and made available for scientific study and then exhibition to the public.

Having worked out the rough shape of a bone, the surrounding rock needs to be cut away to leave a block. This is then wrapped in a shell of paper and strips of cloth soaked in plaster which, once they have hardened, make it possible to remove the entire block and transport it without breaking or disturbing the fossil inside.

The scientific investigation begins in the field, with a detailed note being made of the position of the bones, in order to record how they are arranged on the site and the types of rock that surround them.

The remaining surrounding rock is removed using small tools, or dissolved with acid. Once laboratory preparation is complete, each bone is described, measured, and analyzed in order to identify the animal as precisely as possible and to find out whether it is a new species.

# PRONUNCIATION GUIDE

## A

| | |
|---|---|
| Acrocanthosaurus | ak-row-KAN-tho-SAWR-us |
| Allosaurus | AL-uh-SAWR-us |
| Altirhinus | All-tee-ryne-us |
| Ankylosaurus | ANG-ki-lo-SAWR-us |
| Apatosaurus | a-PAT-oh-SAWR-us |
| Arrhinoceratops | Ay-rye-no-serra-tops |
| Archaeopteryx | ark-eeOP-ter-iks |
| Argentinosaurus | ahy-gen-TEEN-oh-SAWR-us |

## B

| | |
|---|---|
| Baronyx | BAR-ee-ON-iks |
| Brachiosaurus | brack-ee-oh-SAWR-us |

## C

| | |
|---|---|
| Camarasurus | kuh-MARE-uh-SAWR-us |
| Camptosaurus | kamp-toe-SAWR-us |
| Carcharodontosaurus | Kar-kar-owe-don-toe-SAWR-us |
| Carnotaurus | KAR-no-TAWR-us |
| Caudipteryx | caw-DIP-ter-iks |
| Centrosaurus | SEN-tro-SAWR-us |
| Coelophysis | see-law-FYS-iss |
| Coelurus | seel-yur-us |

## Compsognathus / Corythosaurus

| | |
|---|---|
| Compsognathus | komp-so-NATH-us |
| Corythosaurus | cor-IH-thoh-SAWR-us |

## D

| | |
|---|---|
| Deinonychus | dyn-ON-ik-us |
| Dimetrodon | die-MET-roe-don |
| Dimorphodon | die-MORF-oh-don |
| Diplodocus | dip-LOD-oh-kus |
| Drinker | DRINK-er |
| Dromaeosaurus | DROH-mee-oh-SAWR-us |
| Dryosaurus | dry-owe-SAWR-us |

## E

| | |
|---|---|
| Edaphosaurus | ah-DAF-oh-SAW-us |
| Edmontonia | ed-mon-TONE-ee-ah |
| Edmontosaurus | ed-MON-toe-SAWR-us |
| Elasmosaurus | ee-LAZ-moh-sawr-us |
| Eoraptor | EE-oh-RAP-tor |
| Eryops | AR-ee-ops |

## G

| | |
|---|---|
| Gallimimus | GALL-ih-MIME-us |
| Gerrothorax | geh-roh-THOR-ax |
| Gigantosaurus | Jig-a-NOT-oh-SAWR-us |
| Gryposaurus | grip-owe-SAWr-us |

## H

| | |
|---|---|
| Hadrosaurus | HAD-row-SAWR-us |
| Herrerasaurus | he-ray-raar-SAWR-us |
| Hesperornis | HES-per-OR-nis |
| Huayangosaurus | hoo-ah-yang-oh-SAWR-us |
| Hypacrosaurus | high-pah-kroe-SAWR-us |
| Hypsilophodon | hip-sill-owe-foe-don |

## I

| | |
|---|---|
| Ichthyosaurus | IK-thee-oh-SAWR-us |
| Iguanodon | ig-WAN-oh-DON |

## K

| | |
|---|---|
| Kentrosaurus | KEN-troh-SAWR-us |
| Kronosaurus | crow-no-sawr-us |

## L

| | |
|---|---|
| Leaellynasaura | lee-ell-lin-ah-SAWR-ah |
| Leptoceratops | lep-toe-SERR-a-tops |

| | |
|---|---|
| Liopleurodon | LIE-oh-PLOO-ro-don |

**M**

| | |
|---|---|
| Maiasaura | MY-ah-SAWR-ah |
| Megalosaurus | MEG-uh-low-SAWR-us |
| Melanosaurus | mel-uh-NOR-uh-SAWR-us |
| Microceratops | my-kro-SAYR-ah-tops |
| Minmi | MIN-mee |
| Mosasaurus | MOES-ah-SAWR-us |

**N**

| | |
|---|---|
| Nodosaurus | noh-doh-SAWR-us |
| Nothosaurus | no-tho-SAWR-us |

**O**

| | |
|---|---|
| Opthamosaurus | off-THAL-moh-SAW-rus |
| Orodromeus | orrow-drom-ee-us |
| Othnielia | oth-nigh-ell-ee-ah |
| Oviraptor | o-vih-RAP-tor |

**P**

| | |
|---|---|
| Panoplosaurus | pan-oh-ploh-SAWR-us |
| Parasaurolophus | par-ah-SAWR-oh-LOW-fuss |
| Piatnizkysaurus | Pee-at-nits-key-SAWR-us |
| Plesiosaurus | PLEE-see-o-SAWR-us |
| Procomsognathus | pro-comp-son-ay-thus |
| Protoceratops | pro-toe-SERR-a-tops |
| Psittacosaurus | SIT-ah-koe-SAWR-us |
| Pteranodon | ter-an-owe-don |
| Pterosaur | ter-oh-SAW |

**Q**

| | |
|---|---|
| Quetzalcoatlus | kett-zal-coe-at-lus |

**R**

| | |
|---|---|
| Rhamphorhynchus | RAM-for-INK-us |

**S**

| | |
|---|---|
| Saltasaurus | salt-ah-SAWR-us |
| Saltopus | sall-toe-pus |
| Saurornithoides | SAWR-or-nih-THOY-deez |
| Scelidosaurus | skel-ee-doh-SAWR-us |
| Scutellosaurus | sku-TEL-oh-SAWR-us |
| Seismosaurus | size-moh-SAWR-us |

| | |
|---|---|
| Shonisaurus | SHON-e-SAWR-us |
| Spinosaurus | SPINE-o-SAWR-us |
| Stegosaurus | STEG-oh-SAWR-us |
| Stygimoloch | STIG-ih-MOE-lock |
| Styracosaurus | sty-rack-oh-SAWR-us |

**T**

| | |
|---|---|
| Tenontosaurus | ten-on-toe-SAWR-us |
| Thescelosaurus | thess-kell-owe-SAWR-us |
| Titanosaurus | tie-TAN-oh-SAWR-us |
| Triceratops | try-SER-a tops |
| Troodon | TRUE-oh-don |
| Tropeognathus | trop-ee-og-nay-thus |
| Tylosaurus | TIE-low-SAWR-us |
| Tyrannosaurus | TIE-ran-owe-SAWR-us |

**U**

| | |
|---|---|
| Ultrasaurus | ULL-tra-SAWR-us |

**V**

| | |
|---|---|
| Velociraptor | vuh-LOSS-ih-RAP-tor |

# GLOSSARY

**ammonite** extinct marine molluscs, had coiled shells

**ancestor** animal from which a later, related animal has evolved

**ankylosaurs** a group of armored herbivores that lived 76–68 million years ago. There were three main groups of ankylosaurs – ankylosaurids (like Ankylosaurus, see p118–119), polacanthids and nodosaurids "node lizard" (nodosaurids differed from the other two types of ankylosaur that they had spines sticking outward from their shoulders and neck)

**aquatic** water-dwelling

**archosaurs** triassic reptiles, immediate ancestors of the dinosaurs

**binocular vision** ability to focus on the same thing with two eyes

**biped** animal that walks on two hind legs

**bipedal** walks on two legs

**bonebed** site where many fossils from the same time period have been found

**browsing** feeding on high-up leaves, trees, and shrubs

**camouflage** coloring allowing an animal to blend in with its surroundings

**canine teeth** pointed cone-shaped teeth

**carnivore** a meat eater

**carrion** dead body (eaten by scavengers)

**ceratopsian** plant-eating dinosaurs with horned faces

**coelurosaurs** 'hollow-tail lizards' – early members of this group were very small, but its members in the end included the most likely ancestors of modern birds

**cold-blooded** cold-blooded creatures rely on their environment to regulate their body temperature

**conifer** evergreen trees and shrubs

**cretaceous** last period of the Mesozoic era, 135–65 million years ago

**cycad** plant like a palm tree with a middle trunk and leaves

**descendent** animal whose evolution can be traced back to a particular animal or group

**dinosaurs** land-dwelling reptiles from the Mesozoic era

**erosion** the wearing away of the Earth's surface by natural forces

**evolution** process by which one species changes into another, usually over a long period of time

**extinction** the dying out of an entire species

**extinction-level event** catastrophe resulting in the extinction of many species at once (mass extinction)

**femur** main thighbone

**fenestrae** gap or holes in bone, from the Latin for windows

**fern** leafy plant growing in damp places

**fibula** calf bone

**fossil** remains preserved in rock

**geologist** person who studies rock

**gingko** primitive seed-bearing tree with fan shaped leaves, common in Mesozoic era

**grazing** feeding on low-growing plants

**hadrosaurs** duck-billed plant-eating dinosaurs

**herbivore** an animal which just eats plants

**horsetail** primitive spore-bearing plant, common in Mesozoic era

**ichthyosaurs** sea-dwelling prehistoric reptiles

**incisor** tooth adapted for cutting and gnawing, usually at the front of the mouth

**incubate** maintain eggs at good temperature for growth and development

**invertebrate** animal which has no backbone

**jurassic** period of the Mesozoic era, 203–135 million years ago

**Jurassic Coast** area of the coast near Lyme Regis in England, where Mary Anning found many of the fossils that made her famous

**juvenile** young – not yet an adult

**K-T Extinction Event** extinction event which occurred at the end of the Cretaceous period resulting in extinction of the dinosaurs and many other species

**Lesothaurus** Triassic dinosaur

**lizard** scaly-bodied, air-breathing reptile with backbone that evolved from amphibians

**mammal** hairy warm-blooded animal that nourishes young from mammary glands and evolved during Triassic period

**marsupial** mammals that give birth to young which then develop in mother's pouch

**membrane** thin layer of tissue protecting embryo in egg

**Mesozoic era** age of reptiles, 248–65 million years ago which includes Triassic, Jurassic, and Cretaceous periods

**molars** teeth designed for grinding food

**mosasaurs** types of marine reptiles

**omnivore** animal which eats a mixed diet of plants and meat

**ornithopods** beaked, usually bipedal, plant-eating dinosaurs that flourished from the late Triassic to the late Cretaceous (ornithopod means bird feet)

**orthacanthus** a primitive shark

**ossicles** pea-sized bones

**paleontologist** person who studies fossils

**Pangaea** the "super-continent" formed of all Earth's land masses

**paravertebrae** extra bony plates added to backbone of dinosaur

**plesiosaurs** large marine reptiles that lived in Mesozoic era (not dinosaurs)

**predator** animal which hunts other animals to eat

**premolars** teeth behind the canines and in front of the molars

**primates** group of mammals, including monkeys, humans, and their ancestors

**primitive** basic, at an early stage of development

**pterandons** a group of flying reptiles that were usually toothless and had a short tail

**pterodophytes** a type of fern (a plant)

**pterosaurs** flying prehistoric reptiles (not dinosaurs but lived at the same time)

**quadruped** animal that walks on all fours

**rhynchorsaurs** herbivorous reptiles from Mezozoic era

**sauropods** giant, plant-eating dinosaurs with long neck, small head, and long tail

**scavenger** animal that feeds on (dead) meat which it finds, rather than hunts

**scutes** bony protective plates offering defense against attack

**semi-bipedal** sometimes walks on hind legs, at other times walks on all fours

**species** a category of living things, plants or animals, refers to related living things capable of breeding with one another to produce young

**stegosaurs** a group of herbivorous dinosaurs of the Jurassic and early Cretaceous periods, predominantly living in North America and China

**tendons** connect muscle to bone

**territory** the land or area where an animal lives

**thecodonts** ancestors of the dinosaurs

**theropods** fast-moving, bipedal carnivores with grasping hands and claws

**tibia** shinbone

**tree fern** fern with a central trunk

**trackways** footprints preserved in rock as fossils

**triassic** first period of the Mesozoic era, 248–203 million years ago

**vertebrae** the bones which are linked together to make the spine of an animal

**vertebrate** animal with a backbone

**warm-blooded** able to keep the body at constant temperature, regardless of the environment

# INDEX

# ACKNOWLEDGMENTS

**The authors and publishers would like to thank the following people who played such a significant role in creating this Dinosaur Encyclopedia:**

**Illustration**
HL Studios

**Page Design**
HL Studios

**Editorial**
Jennifer Clark, Lucie Williams

**Photo Research**
Sam Morley

**Project Management**
HL Studios

**Jacket Design**
JPX

**Production**
Elaine Ward

All photographs and other illustrations are copyright of USGS, istockphoto, stockxpert, stockxchnge, Flickr.com, except where stated below:

THE NATURAL HISTORY MUSEUM, LONDON

FOSSILIZED DINOSAUR HEART © JIM PAGE / NORTH CAROLINA MUSEUM OF NATURAL SCIENCES / SCIENCE PHOTO LIBRARY

DINOSAUR EXTINCTION © VICTOR HABBICK VISIONS / SCIENCE PHOTO LIBRARY

CONSTRUCTION OF A REPLICA SKELETON OF TITANOSAURUS © PHILIPPE PLAILLY / SCIENCE PHOTO LIBRARY

FOSSILIZED HEAD OF CYNOGNATHUS CRATERNOTUS © SINCLAIR STAMMERS / SCIENCE PHOTO LIBRARY

DINOSAUR TRACKS © OMIKRON / SCIENCE PHOTO LIBRARY

HADROSAURUS / BRONZE SCULPTURE BY JOHN GIANNOTTI, 2003

A Belani, Belgianchocolate, Bernard Price Institute for Paleontological Research Adam Morrel, Kaptain Kobold, Kevinzim, Sarah Montani, Lawrence M. Witmer, PhD, Natuurhistorisch Museum Rotterdam (http://www.nmr.nl/), Striatic, Mark Klingler/Carnegie Museum of Natural History, John Sibbick Illustration, Musée d'histoire naturelle de Fribourg, Suisse, Jarbewowski, Maidstone Borough Council, The Academy of Natural Sciences Philadelphia.